Studying Film at GCSE

The New WJEC Specification

Jackie Newman

David Fairclough Gerard Garvey Julie Patrick

auteur

Acknowledgments/thanks for their help with this book

Jeremy Points, James Clegg, Jack Farmer, Triestina Bozzo and Gioia.

First published by Auteur in 2011
Auteur, 24 Hartwell Crescent, Leighton Buzzard LU7 1NP
www.auteur.co.uk
Copyright © Auteur Publishing Ltd 2011

Design and Setting: Nikki Hamlett at Cassels Design (www.casselsdesign.co.uk)
Stills research: Tom Cabot (www.ketchup-productions.co.uk)
Printed and bound in India by Imprint Digital

British Library Cataloguing-in-Publication Data
A catalogue record for this book is available from the British Library

ISBN: 978-1-906733-57-5

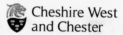

St

The New WJEC Specification

auteur

Note to teachers

Studying Film at GCSE: the new WJEC specification has been produced to support the new specification, assessed for the first time in Summer 2013. The main changes to this specification are:

- the change in genre (from Disaster movies to Superhero movies)
- the replacement of four films outside Hollywood with four new options and
- the change in emphasis of internally assessed work to controlled assessment.

In addition, there have been some slight changes to the requirements for controlled assessment, which we have introduced in response to the experience gained from the first three years of this still relatively new specification. These concern the change in weighting of the industry research and the structure of the production, which is now based on one film idea. Although this book does outline these points and suggest teaching and learning approaches, the authoritative source for all requirements of GCSE Film Studies is the WJEC specification, available on WJEC's website (www.wjec.co.uk – Film Studies – GCSE). We hope the changes we have made will be clear and continue to provide motivation for your students.

As you will be aware, the specification combines study of the Hollywood mainstream – through a set genre – with exploring film produced outside Hollywood. The whole specification is underpinned with opportunities to reinforce learning through creative work. As we know you will want to anchor your course with what most students are familiar with, we have given a lot of space to the new mainstream genre – Superhero movies. This not only represents the most substantial part of the book, it is also informs many of the examples we've used in Part 1 on Film Language. You'll see that we have also tried to give help with ideas for the classroom and some tips for the exam through the 'close up' boxes.

We have, of course, included chapters on two of the new films made outside Hollywood (Mark Herman's *The Boy in the Striped Pyjamas* and Phillip Noyce's *Rabbit-Proof Fence*) and we will be providing resource material for the two other new films – Marjane Sartrapi's and Vincent Parronaud's *Persepolis* and Dennis Gansel's *The Wave*. These will appear on WJEC's website to coincide with the publication of this book.

WJEC's GCSE Film Studies website will also have additional support materials for the new specification and you might also like to know that a new GCSE Film community (teachertalk) is to be found there. This is an opportunity for teachers to 'talk' to other teachers and is an unmoderated site.

You will be aware of the pressures that have led to 'controls' being introduced over internally assessed work at GCSE. In Film Studies, these controls, which are clearly set out in the specification itself, are designed to ensure that you and your students can authenticate the work they produce.

We've been immensely pleased with the enthusiasm both you and your students have shown for Film Studies at GCSE and are already feeling that students are producing some exceptional work, which of course reflects the opportunities you provide for them. We'd like to thank one of those students, Jack Farmer, who provided some of his 'coursework' for use in this book. We wish you the very best in continuing with this course and hope this book will provide you with some additional support.

Jackie Newman, chief examiner, WJEC GCSE Film Studies

Contents

List of Contributors

Jackie Newman was the Director of Media Arts at a large comprehensive in West Yorkshire before retiring in 2009. She is currently the Chief Examiner for WJEC GCSE Film Studies.

Dave Fairclough is Head of Film Studies at Ryburn Valley High School in Halifax and is currently WJEC GCSE Principal Examiner for Paper 1.

Gerard Garvey leads the Arts and Technology Faculty at Rochdale Sixth Form College and is the Principal Moderator for the controlled assessment component of the WJEC GCSE Film Studies Specification.

Julie Patrick is Head of Media Studies at Ryburn Valley High School in Halifax and is the WJEC GCSE Film Studies Principal Examiner for Paper 2.

Introduction

1: *Amélie* (2001)

Watching films can be a magical experience. You can be transported to different countries and new worlds, experience the wildest adventures or become starry-eyed over a favourite star. You can be shocked, become angry, be moved to tears or rocked with laughter. Little wonder, then, that film is seen as the most important art and entertainment form in the world today.

If you love watching and talking about films; if you would like to learn more about how films are made, how they are sold and how they communicate, then this GCSE is for you. If you would like the opportunity to experiment with the wide range of creative and technological processes involved in making and selling films, this course will offer you that. Who knows, it may be the first step in your journey towards an Academy Award or a BAFTA, as director, actor, writer or cinematographer. Certainly, British films like *Slumdog Millionaire* (2008) and *The King's Speech* (2010) have highlighted the countless possibilities open to people working within the film industry today.

This course has been especially designed to build upon what you already know and enjoy about films. You will have the chance to study and discuss films that you have already watched and enjoyed. It will also give you the opportunity to explore films that were not made in Hollywood, films which feature quite different cultures and characters. You will be encouraged to do some research, check out websites like the Internet Movie Database (imdb.com), or Reel Classics (reelclassics.com) before or after you watch a film. They'll help to put the film in its proper historical and social context, and provide bits of trivia that will make the film more fun.

All of us have different tastes when it comes to films, so films are produced to appeal to a wide range of different audiences. Films come in different genres: romance, action, suspense thriller, comedy, animation and horror, to name but a few. You will look at one specific genre – the Superhero movie – in depth.

In terms of your other chosen GCSEs, the study of film can really help to deepen your understanding of subjects such as English Literature, History, Business Studies, ICT, Art, Drama, Photography and Media Studies. It can also provide a 'springboard' into A/S and A Level Film or Media Studies if you wish to take your study of the subject to a higher level.

You will approach GCSE Film Studies via three study areas, which are all connected and work together to give you a strong framework for studying and creating film:

- **FILM LANGUAGE:** those elements that create meaning and how they are organised to tell a story
- **FILM ORGANISATIONS:** the companies that make, sell and exhibit the films we watch
- **FILM AUDIENCES:** how you and other audiences respond to films and how they attract different kinds of audiences.

GCSE Film Studies: course structure and marking

During the time you are studying GCSE Film you will be expected to explore some of the processes involved in the ways films are made and the ways in which they communicate to audiences. You will be expected to produce two main pieces of work in class. These are:

- a film exploration involving two tasks
- a production involving four linked tasks.

This work will be supervised and supported by your teachers and will give you 50% of your overall marks. Towards the end of the course you will complete two written examinations which will account for the other 50% of your marks.

Key terms

Production: The activity of organising the practical and financial matters connected with the making of a film.

Distribution: The processes involved in getting a film to an audience.

Exhibition: Where and how films are shown.

Unit 1: Film Exploration

Task 1: Industry Research (10 marks)

You will begin by exploring a film that you have chosen and then carry out some research into how it was **produced**, **distributed** and **exhibited**. You will then complete a summary of all your research findings (350–500 words).

Task 2: 'Micro' Analysis (20 marks)

After completing your first piece of research on your chosen film you will then think about the way in which the **film's language** is used to create certain meanings and how we respond to those meanings. When you have been asked to study, and then write about, a book or a poem, in English, you read it more than once. Your teacher will ask you to do the same with your film. As with any new area of study, it takes time and practice in order to understand the ways in which mise-en-scène, cinematography, sound and editing (the **micro elements** of film language) can combine to create particular kinds of meanings. Your teacher will make sure that you have plenty of help and lots of opportunities to explore the ways in which film language communicates. After having time to practise, you will then complete an analysis of two of the micro elements of film language in one short sequence from your chosen film (350–750 words).

Unit 2: Production Work

The production consists of **four** linked tasks which are designed to make you think about the ways in which films are created and sold. Before starting this work, you will have completed research on the production, distribution and exhibition of a film that particularly interests you. You will also have completed your 'micro' analysis of a sequence from that film. Now you will have the chance to put forward ideas for a film you will create. You must work on your own and think hard about the target audience for your production. You will begin with Task 1.

Task 1: Creating and Selling an Idea – the Pitch (10 marks)

Your first task will be to create a **'pitch'** for a film you want to make for potential **backers** who might help to fund and produce your film. This pitch will provide the basis for Task 2 (pre-production) and Task 3 (production). Your sales pitch will be about 150 words long and should begin with a '**log line**'. To get a film off the ground you need to have great ideas but you also need the necessary equipment and people who know how to use it. You must also have a potential audience in mind. In order to provide these things you require funding. Potential producers will need to be reassured that your film is going to be a success! You will need to convince them that they will be making a sound investment when they commit to fund your film. Your pitch needs to convey a lot of information in a short time. Investors will need a brief outline of the story and an idea of its genre. They will also want to know your target audience, what other films it is like and who you intend to cast in the leading parts.

Task 2: Pre-production (20 marks)

Once you've completed your pitch you will choose **one** of the following pre-production tasks based on the film you have pitched. You must use

---

Key terms

Film Language: The ways in which a film communicates to its audience.

Micro Elements of Film Language: Mise-en-scène, cinematography, sound and editing.

Key terms

Pitch: A short presentation of ideas for a film delivered to an agent or producer.

Backers: The companies or individuals who provide money to fund a film's production.

Log Line: A one sentence summary of a film.

the appropriate format for your choice and incorporate typical codes and conventions.

- Produce a screenplay for the opening scene of your film (approximately 500 words)

- Create a storyboard using around 20 frames for an important sequence from your film

- Digitally produce a design for a front cover and contents page for a new film magazine that features your film

- Produce a marketing campaign for your film (at least 4 items – for example, a teaser poster, a display item for a cinema foyer and two different types of merchandising).

Task 3: Production (30 marks)

For your production you will be expected to create an accomplished film-based product, based on the ideas you have outlined in your pitch and pre-production task using an appropriate format and typical codes and conventions. For a film sequence you may work in groups of **no more than four** and you must base the sequence on an idea developed by **one** of your group members in their pitch. Also, if you do work in a group, you must be **very clear** about your own role and responsibilities within the group. Your 'evaluative analysis' must also clearly underline **your personal contribution** to the making of the film.

All the other production options must be completed alone and incorporate original images. The options are:

- Creating a short film sequence lasting approximately 2 minutes that creates tension and/or atmosphere (the sequence may be from any section of your film, including a pre-credit sequence that might introduce one or more characters or themes)

- Producing a homepage and at least one further linked page for a website that promotes your film

- Writing and designing a feature, based on the production of your new film, for a film or school/college magazine (the feature should consist of a minimum of 2 pages and include star/director interviews)

- Designing a poster campaign for your new film using at least 3 different posters

- Producing a press pack for your film containing a minimum of 4 items, including at least 2 original promotional still photographs.

Task 4: Evaluative Analysis (10 marks)

Your teacher will ensure that you keep a record of the work you have done in researching, planning and producing your film. You should take time to note down your original ideas and the ways in which they change and adapt as your work develops. Your aim is to make your production work as professional as possible, so it is important that you look carefully at existing examples of your product in order to inform the creative choices you make. When you have completed your production pieces, you will have to reflect carefully on what you have produced and consider what it has helped you to learn about the main study areas – film language, film organisations and film audiences.

The Two Written Exams

Paper 1: Exploring Film

Paper 2: Exploring Film Outside Hollywood

Exploring Film (1 hour 30 minutes) – worth 30%

Your first examination is called 'Exploring Film'. It is worth 30 marks and involves answering four questions focusing on one film genre. You will have spent quite a lot of time in class looking at the 'macro' elements of film language – **genre**, **narrative** and **representation**. You will have considered what the term 'genre' means and its importance in terms of audience, film production and marketing. All the questions set in this examination will focus on Superhero movies. The key to success in this exam is the ability to identify the typical features of the Superhero movie, its **codes and conventions** (for example, **typical** props, themes and camera techniques). Success also depends on your understanding of the target audience and what is involved in producing and marketing these films.

The skills, knowledge and understanding you have gained through your creative work will also have helped you to explore the ways in which Superhero movies communicate to their audiences. You will have studied several Superhero movies in class and will have considered the similarities and differences between the films. You will have looked closely at the ways in which typical patterns can be seen in terms of characters, settings and narrative structures. You will also have become aware of the differences between films which fit into the same genre and have explored the reasons for these differences.

> **Key terms**
>
> **Genre:** A type or category.
>
> **Narrative:** The film's story and the way in which it is told.

> **Key terms**
>
> **Codes and Conventions:** The typical 'rules' of the genre – the micro and macro aspects expected by an audience.
>
> **Typical:** Displaying an expected feature, e.g. a typical feature of the Superhero genre is the character of the Superhero.

Question 1 of the exam – normally in three parts – will relate to a sequence from a Superhero movie. This sequence will be shown three times at the start of the examination. It will usually take about 20 minutes to watch and you will be able to make notes during this time.

Question 2 – also normally in three parts – will be wider-ranging, allowing you to compare the sequence you have viewed with examples of other Superhero movies you have studied.

Question 3 will present you with print-based resource material which relates to the Superhero movie. You will be asked to study the material in order to discuss elements of the marketing and promotion of Superhero films. You will need to analyse the layout, images and text used and comment on why and/or how they have been used. You will also need to consider carefully how this material is designed to appeal to its target audience.

Question 4 – usually in several parts – asks you to demonstrate your knowledge and understanding of the Superhero genre in a creative way. Here, the pre-production and production work you will have already completed will be really useful to you. The tasks for this question will give you the chance to show the importance of genre in terms of how to appeal to audiences and how the concept is put into practice by the organisations which produce and market films.

Exploring Film Outside Hollywood (1 hour) – worth 20%

The second exam will ask you to focus on *at least* one film made outside Hollywood chosen from a set list. You will be given one hour in which to answer three compulsory questions.

Question 1 – normally in three parts – requires you to describe and discuss the sorts of characters, narratives, themes and issues that have been explored in the film you have chosen to study.

In Question 2 – again, normally in three parts – you will be asked to focus carefully on a key sequence from your chosen film, describing in detail the ways in which, for example, important themes and issues are represented. Your understanding of film language gained during the course will help you when answering this question. Even though your chosen film won't be about Superheroes, your genre study will help in that your understanding of how narratives are structured, the identification of specific character types and themes, and the representation of people, places and repeated ideas will all play a part in answering this question.

Question 3 will ask you to respond in a creative way to your chosen film and to show your understanding of the ways in which films target audiences and the way they are marketed and reviewed. You may, for example, be asked to create a blog which talks about your chosen film. You may have to write a review for an existing film magazine. These questions will require you to demonstrate your understanding of film language, organisations and audiences, but it is your personal response to the themes, issues and performances within the film that is really important. Try to remember that film critics do not necessarily like a film they are reviewing, but they usually analyse its language and try to give reasons for the way in which they have responded to the film.

The perfect GCSE for you?

Well, if you love watching and talking about films, this GCSE is perfect for you. Unlike many of the other subjects you study at this level, much of your knowledge and understanding is built up during your leisure time. Every time you go to your local multiplex or municipal cinema, every time you pop to your local video shop for a DVD, every time you settle down to watch a film on television, you are learning more about this subject. The more you learn about specific directors and stars, how films are made and how they communicate, the more pleasure you will get from watching. You'll be able to amaze/annoy your friends and family with your 'insider' knowledge and your ability to predict what comes next. You could make your first creative steps towards becoming the next Tim Burton, Kathryn Bigelow or Quentin Tarantino! We think that over the past hundred years film has become the world's most important art form. We hope that if you don't already agree with us, by the end of your studies, you will.

Chapter 1 Reading Films

- The basic 'language' of film studies and how to use it.
- How we 'read' films rather than just watch them.
- What different devices film-makers use to tell a story.

Introduction

In order to study films you will have to learn about the different ways in which they communicate to an audience – their use of film language. The opening of a film can be very important because it usually introduces the main characters and sets up a problem, or a situation, that in some way needs resolving. It's like the opening of a book – it has to grasp an audience's attention and make them want to find out more about these people, or what is going to happen next.

Close up: the classroom

Watch the opening sequence of any film:

- How does the film-maker try to ensure that an audience will want to watch the rest of the film?
- What different images and sounds help to achieve these aims?
- What is your first impression of the setting and/or characters?
- Does the background music or dialogue affect your first impression?

In many ways, 'reading' a film is just like reading a book but instead of making sense from written words, we make sense of how visual images and sound combine to construct the narrative.

Sitting in the audience you and everyone else will have a unique response to any film that you watch. Although you may not realise it, your response is being guided by film directors. For they will place 'clues' along the way that help you piece together the twists and turns of the story and draw you in to understanding the film from a certain point of view. Just as a writer wants you to feel compelled to finish their book once you have started it, so the director wants you to feel that you can't turn away from the screen; the idea is the same, it's just the techniques that are different.

PART 1 – FILM LANGUAGE

Close up: the exam

Really, the most important part of your studies will be to gain an understanding of film language.

- The study of film is not merely a matter of watching a movie and discussing why you thought it was good or not (although this is very important).

- To express properly a detailed knowledge about films and the way they work, you need a vocabulary in which you can discuss why, and how, a film tells its story.

- To gain the highest possible marks you should understand this vocabulary – film language – and use it appropriately and often.

1: *Rabbit-Proof Fence* (2002)

Close up: the classroom

Look carefully at this image.

- What visual clues are there to the setting and historical time period?

- What appears to be happening?

- Can you guess what kind of film this is?

- Can you start to piece together the plot and how it might be developed?

The setting of the film pictured opposite is clearly isolated and barren. The landscape shows sparse trees and a long dusty road. Straight away we know these girls are being taken against their will and a struggle is taking place. There seems to be nobody around who can help the women and the girls. The clothes the females are wearing clearly contrast with the formal uniform of the officer taking them into the car. They look wild and the colours of their clothes match the colours of the environment, showing they are very much at home and they are about to be taken into 'civilization'.

The officer is centre frame with the smallest girl tucked under his arm nearest the car, so it is more difficult for the older females to try and get her back. His stride is determined, his position strong in contrast to their stooped and straining forms, showing it is unlikely they will win the fight. All the facial expressions we can see are strained, nobody is happy about this situation, yet it is going to happen anyway.

This is the film language at work and you are already demonstrating a sophisticated knowledge of films! But **think**: not all people will read the same things into images and this will be covered later in the book where we consider **different audience readings**.

There are two sections to your studies of film language – **micro elements** and **macro elements**.

Micro elements are:

- Cinematography – the use of the camera

- Editing – the process of putting the shots together after filming

- Sound – music, dialogue, sound effects and voice-overs

- Mise-en-scène – sets and setting, lighting and colour, positioning of characters, body language, costume and make-up, props.

Macro elements are:

- Genre – how we recognise a type of film, e.g. Superhero, comedy – and how they are portrayed

- Narrative – the plot, the story and the way it is told

- Representation – how social groups and issues are 'presented' in a film...how they are 'portrayed'. Representation is a very important aspect of Film (and Media) Studies that crosses the boundaries between macro and micro film language but we treat it as a macro element at GCSE.

Key terms

Frame: Simply put, the camera shot we see on the screen.

Key terms

Narrative: An account of connected events, or 'the story' (the term 'narrative' also refers to the way the story is told, i.e. narrative structure).

Film language: How a film communicates meanings to an audience.

Key terms

Mise-en-scène and lighting: When studying film, lighting is frequently considered to be part of mise-en scène, as in this book. When making films, it's the 'cinematographer' (the Director of Photography) who is responsible for lighting.

The Micro Elements of Film Language

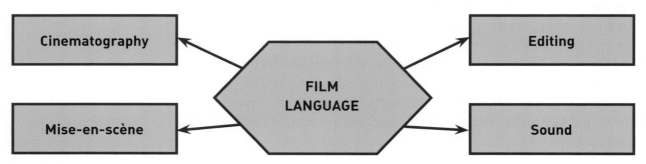

We can recognise the micro elements of film language even in only a short film sequence or in a still image from a film. This is because all the way through a film, the film-makers are creating atmosphere, action or tension by using lighting, sound and camera angles in a particular way. In Film Studies we separate the different micro aspects of film language to help us analyse them, but really they work together to portray the story of the film in a certain way.

Mise-en-scène

This includes:

- setting
- lighting and colour
- positioning of characters within the frame
- body language
- costume and make-up
- props.

All these areas combine to tell audiences where and when the film is set, be it past, present or future. For example, costume and props can give us a clear indication of a historical period. Colour and lighting can create a mysterious atmosphere, and the positioning of characters can tell us a lot about their relationships with each other or how they feel about each other at a particular moment in the film.

Depending on the genre of the film, how accurate the mise-en-scène details are will be of more or less importance. For example an action/ adventure film or comedy may not be as concerned about costume accuracy as a historical or costume drama; though some observers would argue it is always important to represent a place or time in history accurately.

2: *Bend it Like Beckham* (2002)

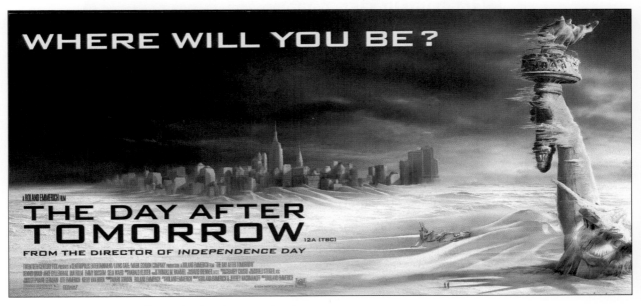

3: *Emma* (1996)

Close up: the classroom

What can you learn about the characters, the setting, the genre of the film and the narrative just from the mise-en-scène of the stills above?

Setting is significant because it is easy to take the setting of a film for granted and not notice the lengths a film-maker has gone to in order to create a sense of the place in which the film is set – whether that be a place relatively familiar to us or a place that is part of another world. We may notice iconic buildings that tell us where a film is set but the finer detail is equally important.

Key terms

Iconic: A readily recognisable image with commonly held associations. Eg, the Statue of Liberty is associated with New York and freedom.

WHERE WILL YOU BE?

A ROLAND EMMERICH FILM

THE DAY AFTER TOMORROW 12A (TBC)

FROM THE DIRECTOR OF INDEPENDENCE DAY

4: The Statue of Liberty still stands, despite a new Ice Age

5: *Alien* (1979) - steely blue space, spaceships and spacemen

6: *The Orphanage* (2007) - shadows, silence and suspense

Close up: the classroom

Create a still for a scene set in: a room in a horror film OR a villain's hideout in an action film. Add in as much detail as you can to create the right kind of atmosphere and to give the audience narrative clues. See the above examples for tips.

As you can see, then, the choices made regarding mise-en-scène are important to creating mood and atmosphere as well as a sense of place.

Lighting and colour can also have a big effect on the atmosphere in a scene. The way lights are positioned focuses our attention on significant props, places or characters. When a scene is brightly lit, this is referred to as **high key lighting** and where there are obvious pools of light and shade this is referred to as **low key lighting**.

Close up: the classroom

Design the homepage for a website dedicated to one film genre. Make sure you consider all genre conventions but especially the use of colour.

Colour can suggest various emotions and moods and is often used for a particular effect. If a certain colour or group of colours is noticeable throughout a film, it is referred to as the film's **colour palette**. Colour can also be used to signify a film's genre.

Look at the posters opposite. How can you tell what genre they might belong to just from the use of colour?

7: *Hostel* (2005)

8: *The Mummy: Tomb of the Dragon Emperor* (2008)

Film posters are an important way that film-makers and cinemas advertise films. They use visual elements of film language to market the film – for example, colour, lighting, positioning of characters. Genre conventions are significant for a successful film poster in addition to the use of stars, directors and intriguing taglines.

Close up: the classroom

Create your own poster for a new Superhero movie taking into account what you have learned.

The other aspects of mise-en-scène to consider are all concerned with characters – how characters are positioned, how they use gesture and body language to express important aspects of the narrative and what they are wearing. **Make-up and costume** are important aspects of a film's mise-en-scène. They can be used to show us a historical period or to help an actor age; but they can also be used to change an actor into an alien or monster!

Mise-en-scène is thus very important. You need to remember how all the different elements in a frame work together to construct a narrative and create atmosphere.

Cinematography

The camera, and how it is used, is a crucial visual tool of the film-maker. It establishes a location by showing a landscape using a long shot at the start of a scene. It captures the reactions and emotions of characters and draws the viewer's attention to the narrative clues we need to piece the story together by the use close-ups on faces or objects. And it can make people look powerful or vulnerable simply by being positioned in a certain place. Even the way the camera moves can determine if the atmosphere in a film is tense or exciting.

It seems obvious to say so, but film is essentially a visual medium. A talented film-maker will use the camera in many different ways to maintain the interest and enjoyment of the viewer. Considering how camera shots and movement are used and what effect these can create will be an important part of your studies.

Sound

Although dialogue is the way the characters communicate with each other and therefore part of how we learn the film's plot, other aspects of sound are important in a film. Sound was not included in films until the late 1920s but even before that music was performed 'live' by musicians to create an atmosphere appropriate to the action taking place on-screen.

Today we are well aware of the importance that music and sound effects generally have on the impact of a film, and technological developments in sound (Dolby, THX, etc.) have greatly enhanced the pleasures received from action-packed films such as the science fiction and Superhero genres.

Just as in the days of live accompaniment, music plays an important role in creating the atmosphere, even helping to define the genre of a film; horror films in particular seem to benefit greatly from the use of suspense-creating musical scores. Changes in pace and volume can affect the emotions of an audience, making them disturbed, amused or very emotional. It can also be important when establishing a specific cultural setting – particularly evident in films like *Rabbit-Proof Fence* (2002) and *Amélie* (2001).

Close up: the classroom

See if you can find (or make) some suitable music to match these actions:

- A woman is walking down a deserted street at night, and she is being followed.

- A Superhero races to rescue a bus full of schoolchildren that has just crashed and is hanging from a bridge.

- A child is re-united with its pet dog after it was accidentally left behind when the family moved house.

Editing

Editing is probably the most important aspect of film creation, though one most of us rarely notice when watching a film. Arguably it is in the editing process where the film actually comes together and this is because the editing process is where film-makers put all the camera shots together.

At this stage the film-makers can decide:

- the order of scenes

- the pace of scenes

- the scenes they will include and discard.

When we look at editing there are two areas to concentrate on:

- the speed of editing (how long each shot lasts)

- the style of editing (how each shot is joined to the next).

It is also significant to consider what aspects of the narrative are being connected together by these edits.

- When two characters are talking, quick cuts are often used between the two faces of the characters talking – why is this?

- When we are looking at a setting the camera tends to move slowly, looking around, and this shot can last a while before an edit – why do you think this is?

The Macro Elements of Film Language

As referred to at the beginning of this chapter, macro elements of film language refer to the 'bigger' issues, the areas of study that bring together your knowledge of cinematography, sound, editing and mise-en-scène.

Genre

Genre refers to the categories that we put films into. We all talk about films in terms of their genre because it is an easy way to refer to films and let people know whether they are likely to enjoy a film or not. If you tell a friend you have seen a great horror film, you are telling them about genre. Straight away they will be making assumptions about what kind of things could happen in that film and whether they would find this thrilling or too frightening to watch! Of course, there are many different types of horror film, so you may need to go into more detail and then you would be talking in a very sophisticated way about film genre.

Close up: the classroom

Complete your own table like the one below with three films that you can think of that fit into the genres listed.

Genre	Film 1	Film 2	Film 3
Superhero			
Crime			
Horror			

Key terms

Generic conventions: The various ways in which film language is typically used within particular genres. For example, most genres use typical settings and props (mise-en-scène), typical characters, typical narratives and typical music.

It is important both for the film industry and audiences to be able to categorise films. We as audiences know what we like and the industry wants to make sure it attracts as large an audience as possible, so marketing devices such as film posters and trailers will follow **generic conventions** that audiences will recognise.

Close up: the exam

- While studying film you will look at a variety of films and discuss what genre they are. But you should remember that genre is not a fixed concept.

- Styles change over time, as film-makers challenge our expectations and society changes its views on how issues and people ought to be portrayed.

- Be conscious that genre as a term is used differently by audiences and the people who actually make films, so what genre a film 'fits into' is always contentious.

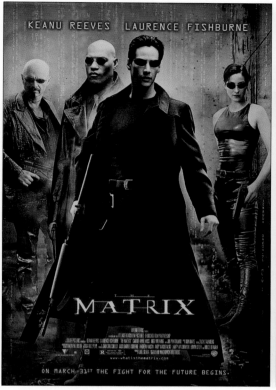

9: *The Matrix* (1999)

10: *The Dark Knight* (2008)

Close up: the classroom

The two posters above are for films from different genres – so why do you think they share so many similarities?

Below are two descriptions of possible scenes from films (not the films above). Discuss in groups what genre you would fit them into and why.

Eventually they stumble into a clearing in the woods. In front of them is an old house and a light shone from one of the windows. As they approach the house they notice the light is a strange, blue colour and it isn't just coming from one window, but glowing in a pulsating rhythm from the whole house...

At last the day had come. 15 years in prison for a crime he didn't commit. He was angry, very angry, and they were going to pay for what they had done to him. He laughed to himself. 'I'm sure it won't come as a surprise to them. After all, they were the ones that trained me.'

You and your friends have probably argued about what genre you would fit these films into. Are they horror? Science fiction? Action? Gangster? Thriller? Of course, you have been given very limited information about the films but this might have made you realise that films don't always fit neatly into one genre, even if this might superficially appear to be the case. Some genres share a number of characteristics so it can be difficult to differentiate one from another at times.

Close up: the classroom

Come up with your own 'film sequences' in small groups. Discuss as a whole class whether they do or don't fit neatly into one genre.

Narrative

The narrative of the film is basically the 'story'. But in the same way as a book we read might go backwards and forwards in time, or start telling part of the story from another person's point of view, so can a film.

Do you sympathise with the main character? Are you given more information than them so that you have a different understanding of events and other characters?

Sometimes a film will just need to set the scene, tell us where we are going or create atmosphere that is important to how we feel at particular points in the story. This is still the narrative at work and unlike the author of a novel, a film-maker is able to use music, sound and special effects to suggest things that, in a novel, are left to our imaginations. Film uses sound and images to create meaning, not just words.

Films use different techniques to show us they are moving to a different part of the story. Sometimes this can be done simply by using editing or colour but sometimes film-makers make audiences work harder to piece a story together.

Close up: the classroom

The Dark Knight is split into clear sections, almost as if different stories are being tied up and then another part of the story begins. Can you trace these different episodes in the film?

Key terms

Narrative structure: The way in which the narrative is ordered and organised within a film.

Narrative voice-over: The use of an unseen narrator to tell the audience parts of the film's story.

Film-makers are able to utilise other techniques to help us follow the story. They might use a **narrative voice-over**, as in *Whale Rider* (2002); or they can even use captions to tell us where the narrative is set in time or place.

Representation

Representation refers to how people and places – fictional or real – are presented to us through various media, in this case film. Films depict how characters in different, often unusual, situations behave and react; but they also carry implicit messages that relate to race, gender and age, which we interpret based on our own cultural and social background and the messages we have received before. Women and men, for example, tended to be represented differently in films made in the 1960s compared to the 1980s – and in some ways differently again in the 1980s compared to today – and we can interpret those representations in different ways. It is also interesting to think about how films produced in different countries offer us different viewpoints, which is something that will be particularly significant in your own study of films produced outside of Hollywood.

Surprisingly, perhaps, Superhero films, which are often based on older graphic novels or comics, do not seem to follow a pattern of changing representations of gender but still offer some very different female characters. For example, the original *Superman* film, made in 1978, presents a strong, working woman in the form of Lois Lane, whereas Mary Jane in *Spider-Man* (2002) seems to be a rather more stereotypically submissive female. And the original *Superman* appeared around 30 years before *Spider-Man*!

Key terms

Representation: how people and places are 'presented' to audiences through the media – the 'image' we gain of them through the way they are portrayed in the media.

Close up: the classroom

Discuss other representations of women in Superhero films you know. Can you begin to explain these representations?

Every film creates meanings for audiences in a variety of ways. Some are directly and consciously expressed, while others are implied. In Media and Film Studies we refer to these two kinds of 'meaning' as **denotation** and **connotation**.

Denotation refers to *exactly* what is shown on screen. So, for example, the opening of *Iron Man 2* denotes Iron Man flying through the sky, landing on a stage surrounded by cheering fans and glamorous women. But the *connotations* of this sequence are that Iron Man (or his alter ego, Tony Stark) is very successful, that he is adored by lots of people and that he is very much enjoying this (female) adulation!

However, every viewer might not see the same connotations, because, as individual members of an audience, we come from different backgrounds, have different beliefs and enjoy different things. So, though most of us

Key terms

Denotation: What we actually see or hear on the screen.

Connotation: The meanings that we may associate with what we see and hear on the screen.

will enjoy the spectacle of this scene, some people may just think the character is horribly arrogant, or they may feel the whole idea is too unbelievable to enjoy.

Close up: the classroom

Watch the opening sequence of *Rabbit-Proof Fence*.

What is denoted in this sequence?

What is connoted about the Aboriginal people that you see in this sequence?

Key terms

Stereotype:
A simplified representation of a person or group of people, repeatedly used so it becomes seen as the norm.

These representations in *Rabbit-Proof Fence* could be seen to be **stereotypical** as they represent Aboriginal people in a way we have often seen them represented in films or television programmes before. They could however be representations that are telling us important things about the culture, beliefs and lifestyle of Aboriginal people in the past.

It is important that you always consider who has made the film you are watching and what messages and viewpoints the film seems to be expressing. You will no doubt see a huge difference between many of the Hollywood films and the films made outside Hollywood you study in preparation for Paper 2, especially in reference to the representation of people from different cultures.

What have we learnt?

This section has been a brief introduction to the way film-makers communicate using 'film language'. Make sure that you can write a short definition of each of the main terms as you will be expected to employ appropriate terminology in your discussion of films – it's really important!

Chapter 2 Mise-en-scène

In this section we will cover:

- How meaning is created through the visual aspects within a frame.
- How the way characters and objects are positioned can provide insights into relationships and narrative development.
- How choices of lighting and colour can create atmosphere and meaning.

11: 'Glad you found time to drop in.' *Spider-Man 2 (2005)*

Look at this still from *Spider-Man 2* – everything you see in this frame can be described as mise-en-scène.

- Where is this scene set?
- Why is this important in relation to what is happening?
- How important are costumes and props in informing us about the characters and the genre of the film?
- What does the colour suggest about what is happening?
- What typical elements of the Superhero genre are evident in this frame?

Mise-en-scène is a French term which was originally used by theatre directors and literally means 'put on stage'. In film, it refers to everything in the scene (either on set or on location) which will appear in the shot. It thus includes:

- the use of lighting and colour
- the sets or setting
- props, costume and make-up
- the positioning of characters within the frame
- body language.

So, when analysing mise-en-scène, there are lots of aspects you need to consider all at once and that is why looking at film stills is a good way to get used to thinking about mise-en-scène. We also need to explore how these different elements work together to create particular kinds of meanings.

Lighting and colour

Lighting and colour are particularly important when signifying mood or atmosphere, as part of mise-en-scène. If woodland is brightly lit with lots of colourful flowers evident, the effect is entirely different from a forest with bare, black trees on a shadowy evening.

If a film is shot in a studio, rather than on location, the following lights are usually used:

- a back light
- a filler light
- a key light.

There are two ways to describe these lighting techniques – 'high key' lighting and 'low key' lighting.

High key lighting refers to the use of a lot of lights to create a colourful and/or bright scene. The 'key light' is the primary light source in a scene. This is a large light often placed beside the cameras. Lighting a subject from behind can be used for a particular effect; for example, it can create a silhouette or a distinctive glow coming from behind a character, which might suggest that a character is mysterious. 'Filler lights' refer to the other lights used in lighting a scene. The director will want to ensure that these 'fill' any gaps in the lighting to avoid the creation of unintended shadows.

Low key lighting is created by using only 'key' and 'back' lights. In doing so, discrete areas of light and shade are created. A film-maker will use this style of lighting to create a particular atmosphere, often associated with particular genres, such as the horror and thriller genres, where a sense of mystery is part of the plot. Low key lighting and flickering candles can also be a feature of a romance.

Key terms

High key lighting: Bright lighting, the addition of lots of artificial light to a scene.

Low key lighting: Where fewer filler lights are used creating shadows and pools of darkness.

So lighting and colour are used for two main purposes – to set the mood of a scene but also to give the film a particular 'look' that might provide a visual clue to how we 'read' the film.

A director will often have a clear idea of how they want colour to work in a scene, as colour can have an impact on our emotions and therefore on how we understand a scene. Films can often use a particular colour palette, which can relate to the genre or to the director's style. Superhero films are a good example, as these often use strong, primary colours to reflect the comic book and graphic novel origins of the genre.

Colour can be used **symbolically**. For example, what do you think of if someone asks you to think of the colour red? What do you associate with the colour white? Your response to these questions may be influenced by your own background, as different cultures have different associations with colours. And again, the Superhero genre often uses colour symbolically, using these cultural connections to identify heroes and villains.

Key terms

Symbolic: An image or object which has additional meaning or cultural significance.

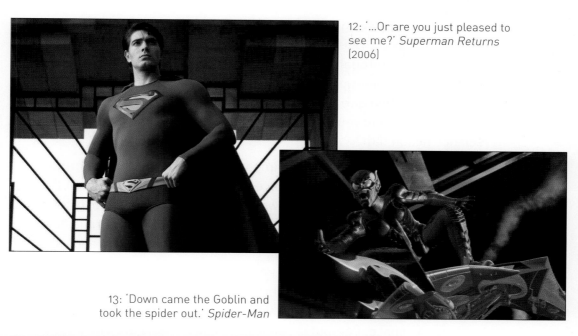

12: '...Or are you just pleased to see me?' *Superman Returns* (2006)

13: 'Down came the Goblin and took the spider out.' *Spider-Man*

Close up: the classroom

Compare the colour in the costumes of these characters from different Superhero films. Is it clear who the villain is and who is the hero **from the use of colour**? How has your knowledge of film and your cultural knowledge influenced your decision?

Close up: the classroom

This is a still from the film *The Wave* (2008).

14: *The Wave*

How would you describe the use of lighting in this shot?

- Why do you think the cinematographer has lit this scene in this way?

- What clues are there to what is happening in the narrative at this moment?

Sets and Setting

The location and design of the set is very important to our enjoyment of a film. We can get whisked away to another universe or even to a place of total fantasy through the use of a particular setting (though of course, costume and make-up are going to play a big part in this too). Some aspects of setting give us huge clues to the genre of the film straight away – what would you expect to see in a Western for example, or in a science fiction film?

Sometimes the setting plays an important part in the film's narrative. For example, in *Rabbit-Proof Fence*, the narrative is largely about the colonisation and the tension between the Aboriginal and British cultures. Showing how both groups lived and worked in Western Australia during the 1930s is therefore very important to the film's messages and values.

The setting of a film is also very important as it allows the film-maker to impress audiences with wonderful landscapes, large crowds, huge spaceships and fantastic, futuristic worlds. It also tells us where we are in time and space. Computer generated visual effects are often used to maximum effect in set design. For example, instead of employing vast amounts of extras for a film, computer technology can now create artificial crowds.

Props, Costume and Make-up

Costume generally works alongside setting to establish a film's narrative in a certain time and place. Though we may not have first-hand knowledge of the clothes worn by eighteenth century pirates, we expect films to represent these characters with a certain degree of accuracy.

Again costume can use colour symbolically to give us clues about a character's mood or role in the film. It is also important to tell us what genre we are watching. Make-up in film is more than simply just about glamour. Consider for example the hours in make-up this actor had to endure!

15: 'Come to Freddy.' *A Nightmare on Elm Street* (1984)

Costume and make-up together can have a lot of impact on the atmosphere of a scene, and props are often focused on to give us big clues about the narrative and what is going to happen soon. If a close-up shot of a gun is used just before someone has had an argument, the audience will make the connection that this argument is about to turn nasty.

Costume can change in films as a way of telling us something about different characters. A change in costume throughout the film can suggest that things are changing for characters within the narrative.

Costume, then, simply refers to the clothes worn by a character, be it the mud-spattered armour of a Middle-Earth warrior or the breathtaking dress of a fairytale princess. It can be used to signify wealth, what job a character does or what period the film is set in.

In some cases costume is actually a necessary component of the genre and the narrative, and this is particularly important to the Superhero genre as Superheroes often have to hide their identity. Batman, for example, uses costume both to mask his identity and to enable him to fight crime. The X-Men (and Women) don their 'uniforms' when going into action and working together as a team.

Close up: the classroom

Compare the two images from *Hancock* (2008).

16: 'People don't like you, *Hancock*.'

17: Superhero

Hancock is transformed by his newly acquired PR man, Ray Embrey, into the 'typical' Superhero by his costume.

- Compare the differences between the old Hancock and the Superhero he is trying to be.

- What aspects of costume, colour and physical expression differentiate the new and old Hancock?

- Are there any connections between the old and new Superhero?

Costume doesn't just tell us about historical time but can also tell us what time of day it is and what people are doing. How could you show it was a Sunday morning in the city as opposed to a Monday, just from the costume characters were wearing? How would you establish 'the boss' in an office setting?

In *Rabbit-Proof Fence* it is actually the costume that gives us clues to the girls' lifestyle. They don't wear shoes and their clothes are the same colour as the earth around them – what does this tell us about them and the lives of the Aboriginal people at the time in which the film was set?

18: Following the rabbit-proof fence

Make-up

In everyday life, a discussion about make-up may lead you to think about women wearing it in order to look more attractive; but in films make-up can be used to make actors look hideous, or much older. Make-up can create aliens from fantasy worlds or recreate historical figures from our past, and it is also very important for creating scars and injuries. Make-up can even change an actor's on-screen gender, as in *The Nutty Professor* (1996) or *Mrs Doubtfire* (1993).

Characters: Positioning and Body Language

Characters can be positioned within the frame to show their relationship with each other. For example, if two characters are falling in love, they may be placed close together, with the jilted partner in the centre of the frame behind them scowling!

Body language informs us of the different relationships between the characters on-screen. We are used to reading certain gestures and 'looks' that carry meaning within our culture. Obviously, when watching films from other cultures you may have to learn about other gestures, such as the use of bowing in Japanese culture.

Close up: the classroom

- What do you notice about the positioning of the two main characters in this still from *The Boy in the Striped Pyjamas* (2008)?

- Why has the director positioned the boys in this way? What does it tell us about their situations?

- Do setting and costume also add to the meaning in this still?

19: The first meeting. *The Boy in the Striped Pyjamas* (2008)

Body language can also show status or emotion so we look for these clues in films too. The hero in an action or Superhero film will have a strong stance. A weaker character might show they are nervous by fidgeting.

Often the characters are balanced within the frame by the film-maker's careful positioning. People may be placed at different heights to show their status within a scene. If a character is positioned in the foreground and in focus, then in 'reading' the shot we assume there is something very important about them that we need to pay attention to, even though it may be a character in the background or out of shot who is talking.

Although elements of mise-en-scène are separated for analytical purposes, the different parts combine together to create an overall effect; you should always consider all the different elements as part of one whole.

Mise-en-scène links closely to genre conventions. For example, if you consider the science fiction genre you will have various expectations of the mise-en-scène. You might expect low key lighting if it has a dark, frightening aspect; but also, because of their scientific, technological elements, you can also expect to see bright white or metallic colours.

Mise-en-scène plays a big part in creating the appropriate setting for a film and the right kind of atmosphere. It gives audiences clues as to how the narrative is going to develop.

Every element of a visual image can carry meaning. The position of elements within an image, colour and lighting, camera shots and movement all affect the way we interpret what we see.

Close up: the classroom

- Design a storyboard for a sequence on a spaceship in a science fiction movie. Ensure you consider character positioning, set and lighting as a way of showing significant characters and aspects of the narrative.

- Design a film poster for a new Superhero movie, ensuring your use of costuming and positioning of your characters shows a heroic stance and a clear sense of 'heroes and villains'.

Chapter 3 Cinematography

In this section we will cover:

- How the camera is used to show the narrative from a particular point of view.
- How the camera is used to emphasise atmosphere and emotions.
- The specific terminology used to describe camera shots and movement.

When exploring cinematography, it is important to look at the director's choice of shot and camera movement. Shot duration (how long each shot lasts), movement and framing can tell us a lot about characters, action and relationships. What we are shown determines whose point of view we see events from and might provide us with clues about what will happen later.

In discussing camera framing we are looking at what we can see within the frame of the cinema, or television, screen. Framing can draw our attention to the characters' emotions by focusing on their faces, or on the other hand it can show us dramatic landscapes by placing us much further away. In this section, we are going to show how the different ways in which the camera is used can create different meanings for viewers.

Camera shots

Each time a camera focuses on something a camera shot is used. For example, a close-up, mid-shot or low-angle shot; and these shots are chosen by film-makers at particular moments in the film to show us events in a certain way. These shots help to create meaning and so lead audiences to read the event in a particular way.

You will already have a good understanding of how these shots can create meaning without even thinking about it, because you are used to reading films in a visual way. For example, a close-up shot is often used to focus our attention on one particular thing. This is often a character's facial expression because people's reactions to events are one of the most important parts of most films' narratives. It is through their reactions that we feel the dramatic moments of the action – such as fear, love and anger.

Key terms

Close-up shot: When we are close up to a subject so we can focus on a face, or an object in detail.

Significant prop: An object in a scene that our attention is drawn to because it is going to become of significance later on in the film.

A **close-up** can also focus our attention on a significant prop. If there is a sudden close-up of a knife on a kitchen table during a scene where a pair of characters is violently arguing, we should probably prepare ourselves for more violence!

An **extreme close-up** shot focuses the audience's attention on minute detail, often intended to jar or shock the viewer through artistic effect rather than for particular generic conventions. The tight framing of the extreme close-up can create a sense of discomfort and can really make us feel that there is no escape from this dramatic emotional reaction, or frightening situation.

20: *Spider-Man*

21: *The Blair Witch Project* (1999)

Close up: the classroom

Explain how these different close-up shots create meaning for audiences.

In contrast, a **long shot** of a character enables us to see the entirety of their body language and costume. Costume is often hugely important in the Superhero genre and so is large-scale action. Therefore, long shots are going to play a big part in this genre, particularly when combined with a wide angle, creating sweeping vistas or cityscapes for Superheroes to fly around in and fight villains.

Long shots used in combination with a wide angle camera lens establish a clear sense of place; hence the term '**establishing shot**'. Establishing shots are often used at the beginning of films, and sometimes at the start of every scene if the setting is of particular importance to the genre. If the director wants us to take in the surroundings, they might pan the camera around as well. Adventure films, for example, often have exotic settings so the film might start with a pan around a noisy, dense jungle or an instantly recognisable ancient city.

A long shot may also be needed to offer perspective. For example, in *Superman 2* (1980), many long shots are used when Superman has to fight three criminals from his home planet (see picture below) as this shows us how their 'fight' affects ordinary people on a very large scale. As long shots often give us more background to look at the setting becomes more important to the action.

> ### Key terms
>
> **Long shot:** When we are a distance away from the subject so all of it is visible, as is maybe more of the setting and other people.

22: A city in danger.
Superman II (1981)

Sometimes this is because the setting is important to that character. For example, we often see long shots of Simba from *The Lion King* (1994) in his natural habitat because it is such an important part of the narrative.

A long shot might also be used to show us a group of characters – to show us an intimidating gang or a large group of people trying to escape something.

A **mid-shot** shows us a character from the waist upwards and is often used so we can focus on the dialogue between two or more characters. It may show the setting as well, but usually not so much that it stops us from focusing on the dialogue or action.

23: Mother and son. *The Boy in the Striped Pyjamas*

Close up: the classroom

Watch the skydive sequence in *Iron Man 2*.

- How important are the use of long and wide shots to this sequence?

- How important is the setting to the action?

- Why and when are close-ups used?

Key terms

Low angle: If the camera is positioned below a subject looking up, it looks larger and more powerful.

High angle shot: When a camera is positioned above a person or object, it generally looks smaller and so more vulnerable.

A **high angle shot** is when the camera is placed above the subject and a low angle shot is the opposite. When the camera is placed higher up than a subject or person, we feel we are looking down on them. This can make them look smaller and less important or weaker. Conversely, if the camera is at a **low angle**, the character looks bigger, making them stronger. Monsters are seen to loom over us; or the shot may be just to show a tall skyscraper to remind us of a city's wealth and modernity.

Low angle and high angle shots do not always show weakness or strength. Have a look at these examples of high and low angle shots – what meaning do these images from *Kick-Ass (2010)* create?

24: 'It's time to get the bad guy.' *Kick-Ass*

25: 'With no power comes no responsibility.' *Kick-Ass*

Also, when Spider-Man is whizzing through the city sky, swinging from building to building, the camera moves alongside him, sometimes above and sometimes below. This is not to show him as alternately vulnerable or powerful; it is to make the audience feel that they are alongside him, joining in with his adventures.

When analysing aspects of film language such as cinematography, it is important that you use your broader knowledge of film too. The way the camera is used tells us particular things about the narrative and may fit in with conventions of a particular genre; so you should always analyse a micro aspect of film language in the context of the film you are studying.

Key terms

Steadicam: A camera mounted on a harness that is then attached to camera operator, so the movement of the camera is smooth.

Hand-held camera: The camera is held manually. Shots are therefore less clear as the camera is held without support.

Camera movement

Developments in camera technology mean that a director of contemporary films can move the camera around in various ways to change an audience's experience of the images presented. The introduction of the **Steadicam** allowed a smooth shot even when the camera operator was moving quickly.

If a director doesn't want the smooth camera movement the Steadicam allows, they might choose to use a **hand-held camera**. The more 'rough and ready' effect of using a hand-held camera makes the audience feel that the action is somehow more 'real', in part because we associate the hand-held camera with the documentary genre and news footage. Action sequences in modern film and scenes where characters are being pursued use this technique to bring audiences closer to the action, although sometimes at the risk of confusing them if the scene is not carefully edited.

There are many different ways a camera operator can move the camera and this obviously allows us to see the action from different viewpoints. It isn't only Steadicam or hand-held cameras that give the effect of movement; cameras can be put on tracks (tracking shots), on cranes (crane shots), on cars and trucks and even in helicopters (commonly used for bird's eye view shots, perhaps to introduce a city-scape or follow the progress of a high-speed pursuit). Action films will usually use a combination of these.

Zooming in and out

Zooming in and out is not officially camera movement, as it is only the camera lens that is moving. But it is a camera technique that brings us closer to the action or, when appropriate, pulls us away from it. The camera could quickly zoom out from a character, emphasising their isolation and despair or zoom in to a character to make their entrance into the scene more dramatic, for example.

Close up: the classroom

Create a storyboard sequence for a Superhero film, using as many of the camera angles and movements discussed as you can.

- How does using lots of camera movement affect your sequence in terms of pace?

- Compare your storyboard to others. Did you all come up with similar or different uses of the techniques?

Canted frame, bird's eye view and framing

Other camera techniques you should look out for include the **canted frame**, which is when the image in the frame is at an angle, which means that the camera was at an angle when the shot was filmed. This strange angle makes the audience feel disorientated.

26: Canted frame – *Watchmen* (2009)

A **bird's eye view** shot is taken by the camera looking straight down onto a setting or person, so we are witnessing the action directly from above. This can be used to show us we are watching someone but may well just show us a setting or landscape from a different perspective. Cities are often shown to us from this angle, to emphasise their size and to show us the setting form an exciting angle, which looks particularly good in a cinema.

27: Bird's eye view– of the planet! *Superman Returns*

Framing refers to the edges of the shot. What has been deliberately selected for – or excluded from – the frame relates closely to camera shots. However, we often talk of the 'tight framing' of a sequence, by which we usually mean a sequence of close-up shots where little of the mise-en-scène is noticeable. Our attention is focused where the frame seems to fit tightly around the characters, adding discomfort to our viewing experience because the characters also feel uncomfortable.

Close up: the classroom

Watch the opening of *Rabbit-Proof Fence*.

- Consider the effect of the bird's eye view shot.
- Why has the landscape been filmed in this way?

Depth of field

Depth of field refers to the focus of the camera lens. A director might want to draw our attention to particular objects or characters within a shot, so they will make other elements look slightly out of focus or even completely blurred. Usually our attention is being drawn to characters in the foreground so when this is different, it creates an interesting visual effect. Sometimes directors blur the setting and focus on a character further away in the shot. This is referred to as **shallow focus**. In some instances, however, the setting, colours and the landscape are often very important to the narrative, so then the director will want every detail to be sharp and in focus.

To gain a deeper understanding of camera shots it is important to analyse sequences from different genres and to practise framing with the camera yourself. Make sure you create storyboards using camera shots and take actual photographs using your classmates as subjects. If you consider some of the things explored in the genre chapter, you will see that certain genres will use cinematography in particular ways as part of the recognisable conventions of that genre, so think about your understanding of generic conventions before embarking on storyboarding and filming.

Close up: the classroom

Task 1

- Watch the opening of:
  - a Superhero film
  - an action adventure film
  - a horror film.

- Analyse and compare how each sequence uses camera angles and movement to draw audiences into the narrative of the films.

- How can you tell who the main characters are straight away?

- To what props is your attention being drawn?

- How are camera angles being used to reveal different aspects of the narrative?

Task 2

- Storyboard your own short sequence for a film from a particular genre using only photographs.

- Present the sequence to the class and see if they can work out:
  - who the main characters are and what their relationships are to each other
  - the genre of the film
  - what is going to happen after this sequence.

Chapter 4 Editing

In this section we will cover:

- What is editing?
- Ordering shots – which shot follows which?
- Style of editing – how each shot is joined to the next.
- Pace of editing – how long should each shot last?

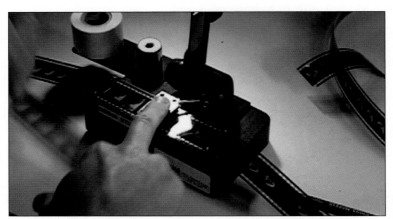

28: In the cutting room

Introduction

Key terms

Editing: The process by which shots are put together into sequences or scenes. Usually described according to rhythm or pace (i.e. the varying lengths of the shots in the sequence) and type of transition (e.g. cut, fade, dissolve, mix, wipe).

Editing simply means where one shot is slotted next to another to form a sequence. A shot is the amount of film between two edits; it can vary in length from a few seconds to (in some exceptional cases) a few minutes, although most shots are measured in seconds. A sequence is a group of shots edited together to show a distinct event or events in a film.

The process of editing involves looking at all the footage which has been shot during the making of the film (raw footage), placing it in the desired order and physically joining it together. This used to involve cutting up the raw footage and sticking it together; this is where the terms 'cutter' and 'cutting room' come from. These days the physical process is done digitally using computer software, but the principles that underlie the process remain the same.

It was not long before early film-makers realised how editing could have a great effect upon the audience and wasn't just about joining together the film footage to run it through the projector. Relatively early on film-makers realised that a clumsy edit could 'jolt' the audience and remind them they were watching a film, spoiling their attempt to immerse the audience in the story. To avoid this, the classical style of Hollywood editing (or **continuity editing**) was developed, the rules of which are still used today. This style of editing was designed to be smooth and make sure that an audience barely noticed the transition from one shot to the next.

Other pioneering film-makers, especially the early film-makers from Russia (see below), experimented with the power of editing and its uniqueness to film. They developed an approach where the edits not only drew attention to themselves but created a greater level of meaning too.

To this day editing remains one of the most powerful tools at the film-maker's disposal and continues to develop and be a subject of sometimes furious debate, especially regarding its pace. If you make your own film, editing will be where your film takes shape and its needs should be uppermost in your mind from the very earliest stages of planning your film.

The three areas to consider are:

- Order of edits – which shot follows which?

- Style of editing – how each shot is joined to the next.

- Pace of editing – how long does each shot last?

We will be looking at each of these areas in more detail to see how this sometimes 'invisible' skill has great power for film-makers. Film editing is the only process that is unique to cinema and which separates film-making from all other art forms that preceded it, such as photography, theatre and dance.

29: A modern editing suite

Close up: the classroom

Look at a film trailer and:

- Try to count up all the different shots.

- Discuss what effect the trailer is designed to have and how editing helps to create it.

Order

The order of shots and sequences at its most basic must allow the audience to understand the film. The editing must place the events of the film in the right order to reflect how the narrative unfolds. Although different narrative structures and flashbacks allow flexibility in this, a film will usually follow a chronological structure. For example, we may not want to reveal the murderer in the first scene if the film is about trying to figure out who they are.

Aside from this 'common sense' consideration, the order we choose to put the shots in can exert a more subtle and a much more powerful effect. This arises from association or suggestion: if we continually edit a character into dark scenes of evildoing it will not take long before we create the impression that this character is a villain.

Russian film-makers of the 1920s realised how powerful these choices could be. Sergei Eisenstein, perhaps the most famous, talked about how he could use his 'cine-fist' to punch through to the audience with the force of his messages; the power of this came from his use of editing. Eisenstein realised that editing could create meanings in many different ways (especially in silent film where the visual was all important). They thought that image A cut together with image B did not just create image AB but a third meaning, C. For example, if we join an image of a car (A) and a road (B) together we may think of a journey (C); if we join the same image of a car (A) and a gravestone (B) together we may imagine a car accident (C). This style of editing and its different applications became known collectively as **montage editing**. These days the term montage is more commonly used to describe a series of images that summarise events in a shorthand fashion. However, the process of communicating a lot of information or meaning very quickly can be derived from Russian film-making. A very famous experiment to show the power of montage editing was conducted by Lev Kuleshov.

Key terms

Montage Sequence: A series of shots which summarise an action or build a mood, rather than playing it out in the equivalent of real time (Source: BFI).

The Kuleshov Effect

In his experiment, Kuleshov edited together the same image of an actor's face with a bowl of soup, a body in a coffin and an attractive woman. Although the actor's expression remained unchanged, the audience's reaction to the shots was different each time they viewed his face. The audience 'raved about the acting': the hunger he felt looking at the soup, the sorrow at the coffin and the attraction he obviously felt for the young woman. All of this was despite the fact that his expression remained unchanged. Kuleshov used the experiment to indicate the usefulness and effectiveness of film editing. The implication is that viewers brought their own emotional reactions to this sequence of images. For us it shows how much potential meaning there can be in any editing choices we make.

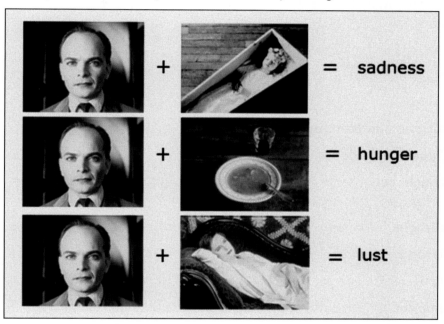

30: The Kuleshov Effect

Close up: the classroom

Compile two or three sheets of clip art images and cut them up into separate images.

- See how many different meanings and stories you can create using the same images.

- See if the rest of the class can work out what you have tried to do.

So, as we can see, the choices we make when editing can have very powerful effects. The skill is to try and control these effects to convey the meanings we intend.

Close up: the classroom

Log onto the Film Education website.

Go to http://www.filmeducation.org/thor/index.html

- Use their *Thor* trailer activity to see how you can use editing to make trailers with different meanings.

Style

Style of editing is about how we choose to join one shot to the next and the effect we wish this to have on the audience. There are two areas to consider:

- transitions and matches
- passage of time.

Transitions and Matches

Main Types

- a **straight cut** – where one shot is joined straight to the next with no effect and as little 'disruption' as possible
- a **fade-out** – where the screen fades to black
- a **dissolve** – where one image is slowly brought in beneath another one
- a **wipe** – where one part of the screen moves to wipe across the other
- a **jump cut** (smash cut) – where the audience's attention is brought into focus on something very suddenly
- a **cutaway** shot (usually a close-up) – used to focus on a significant object or the focus of the character's attention.

Uses

The most common transition in editing is the straight cut. We are so used to seeing these that we generally do not notice them. Fades will often signify the ending of an episode in the film. Dissolves will create a blending of the two scenes into each other. A wipe and a jump cut will be instantly more noticeable to our eyes, drawing our attention immediately to a character or object that appears on-screen directly after the edit. A cutaway is used to control the audience's attention: if we see a cutaway to a knife it could foreshadow a murder or the cutting of a cake!

Matches

When editing a sequence an editor will try to make transitions smoother, or less noticeable, by looking to 'match' one shot to the next, where the similarities are used to smooth out the transition or establish a connection. These can be matched on sound, action, colour or gesture.

The film-maker can choose to place the shots in a certain order so as to create a smooth visual transfer from one frame to the next. When two consecutive shots are matched in terms of the way they look, this is called a graphic match. When sound 'overlaps' two shots to smooth their transition, this is known as a sound bridge. Similarities in gesture, motion, action and colour can also be used to smooth the transition between shots.

Passage of time

Editing can be used to show the passage of time and to set the pace of a film. Wipes, dissolves, fade-ins/outs are used to demonstrate the passage of time between shots and sequences. Clocks are not always featured in films to tell us that time has passed! It is all down to the editing and the way the shots are slotted together.

Pace

The number of shots or edits in a sequence will determine its pace. The fewer the number of shots used in a sequence the more relaxed the pace will feel. Longer shots can be used to build up tension as the audience waits for 'the moment' to be broken by the next edit. When a film-maker makes us jump it quite often will be achieved through the use of a jump cut after a relatively longer shot.

Where the length of shot shortens and the number of edits increase, the pace of the film will speed up. This is most often associated with action and excitement to simulate the visual confusion that we feel when lots of things are happening quickly or at the same time. A criticism of many modern blockbusters is that this pace has become too fast leading to genuine disorientation and confusion that spoils the film and ability to effectively 'take it all in'.

Close up: the classroom

Watch the sequence from *Spider-Man* (2002) where Peter Parker is deciding how he will use his powers, designing a costume and trying out his webbing (approximately 32m–34m).

- What name do we usually give to this kind of sequence?
- What transitions are used?
- What effect do they create?
- When does the pace of the editing change and why?

Conclusion

We have only considered the basics of editing here but even so it has shown us what a powerful tool it is for the film-maker. If you want to really understand how film has the effect upon us that it does then you should think about how a film is cut together as you watch films. If you can use this knowledge in your short film then it will be a much more effective piece.

Close up: the classroom

The aim of this task is to show how editing can create different meanings and stories.

- In groups of 3, take 10–15 images with a stills camera.
- Use different camera angles, framings, distances and shots of you doing things or making different facial expressions.
- Then create 2–3 different storyboards (you could use Windows Movie Maker or Power Point) using the same images but in different orders. Write a paragraph for each different narrative explaining what is happening.
- See if your classmates can follow your different narratives.

Close up: creative work

Whenever you film, you should always think about how it will be edited.

Always film enough at the start and end of your shot.

Film everything two or three times, from different angles, then you will have more creative choices when you put it all together in editing.

Think about cutaways to show significant items or just to illustrate what the character is looking at.

Chapter 5 Sound

In this section we will cover:

- What is sound?
- What elements make up a film's soundtrack?
- How can we use these sounds in different ways?
- Why is sound so important?

31: Sound recording in the early days of cinema

Key terms

Sound or Soundtrack:
The sounds that can be heard in a film – dialogue, sound effects, music.

Sound is all the things we hear when watching a film. Although dialogue is an important aspect of most films' narratives (because it moves the story on), we also concentrate on how music and sound effects are used.

Sound was not included in films until the late 1920s but it was still important for creating an atmosphere in films and was created in cinemas by live musicians. Nowadays we fully understand the importance music and sound effects have on the impact of a film. Developments in media technology, such as surround sound, have greatly enhanced the pleasures received from action-packed films such as the action and Superhero genres.

Music often plays a vital role in creating the appropriate atmosphere in films; horror films in particular seem to benefit greatly from the use of suspense-creating musical scores. The change in tempo and volume can greatly affect the emotions of an audience and the style of music can make audiences scared, amused or very emotional.

The Soundtrack

A film's soundtrack can be divided into three main components:

- Dialogue
- Sound effects
- Music.

Dialogue – the lines spoken by the characters on-screen. When the lines are spoken off-screen this is usually referred to as a voice-over.

Sound Effects – those sounds added to the soundtrack to enhance the action or emphasise an action. They are created by a **Foley artist** (named after sound pioneer Jack Foley). They can be the obvious things like gunshots and stabbing sounds but they also include the more 'run of the mill' sounds such as footsteps and equipment noises. Other sound effects created in post-production by the sound designer are sometimes referred to as 'atmos. effects', the sound effects used to generate a certain atmosphere – e.g. a howling wind.

Music – this can be the score or the soundtrack. A score is the music which is written for a specific sequence. The soundtrack may feature pre-existing songs selected as they fit the meaning of the sequence and they may even be songs written specially for the film.

Key terms

Foley Artist: Foley is the reproduction of everyday sounds for use in film-making. These reproduced sounds can be anything from the swishing of clothing and noise of footsteps to squeaky doors and breaking glass.

32: The modern approach to sound recording

Using Sound

So far we have only really described the types of sounds we might hear. These three components can be used in the many ways which we will consider below.

Diegetic and Non-diegetic Sound

- Diegesis – the world of the film as we see it on-screen. The place where the story unfolds and the characters exist.
- Diegetic Sound – sound which is part of the world we are watching, e.g. dialogue, a car engine.
- Non-diegetic sound – sound which is NOT part of the world we are watching, e.g. voice-over, background music or score.

On-Screen and Off-Screen Sound

- On-screen sound – where we can see the source of the sound, e.g. a gun fired by an actor.
- Off-screen sound – where we cannot see the source of the sound, e.g. a wolf howling in the night.

Parallel and Contrapuntal Sound

- Parallel Sound – where the sound we hear complements the picture we see. This type of sound is what we would expect to hear, it 'goes with' the action, e.g. a very moving orchestral piece for moments of high emotion.
- Contrapuntal Sound – where the sound we hear does not fit the pictures we see. Often used by the film-maker to make a point or different meaning related to the action. Sometimes used to foreshadow change or tell us something is about to happen, e.g. sad music played over a happy moment.

Sound Bridges

Sound bridges are where the sound continues from one scene to the next, even if the pictures do not. This is used to ease transition or create a sense of continuity. Examples could be the sound of a car taking us from one place to the next or when music overlaps two scenes to link them.

Close up: the classroom

Analyse the sound in the opening sequence from *Watchmen* (2009):

- To what effect is the sound used? What do you think and feel?
- Is there a sound bridge? Where?
- Where does the same sound go from diegetic to non-diegetic? How?
- Which sounds are parallel? Which are contrapuntal? Do they change?
- Is there any on-screen or off-screen sounds? What are they?
- How important is sound in this sequence?

Conclusion

Sound has become indispensable to the film experience. It enhances what we see and increases the effect and size of the things we don't see. We need to be able to assess all the different kinds of sound and how and why this 'sound design' creates the effect it does.

Close up: the classroom

- Think about and plan carefully the sound for your film.
- Try to use all three elements of dialogue, sound effects and music.
- Don't just use a song by itself – this is not a pop video but a short film.
- Consider what you think the audience should hear for every single shot to help create the meaning(s) you want.

Chapter 6 Narrative

In this section we will cover:

- The different ways a story can be structured.
- Narrative viewpoints.
- How audiences are positioned by the narrative.
- How film-makers manipulate time in order to shorten and lengthen the passing of time in the narrative.

33: 'These are the old days, the bad days, the all-or-nothing days.' *Sin City* (2005)

To talk about a film's 'narrative' is to consider how the 'story' of a film is constructed in the film, as well as the actual story itself. As part of your studies of narrative, you will thus need to consider the order in which a film's events are told – the narrative structure – and from whose point of view we are meant to observe these events.

Generally, narratives are driven forward by some sort of action and this is usually the actions of the main characters.

Activity Box

Look at the opening of *Sin City*.

- Who is narrating the story?
- Why do you think a narrator is being used?
- What does this add to the film?

Narrative structure

These are the three common ways in which a film narrative can be structured:

1 Circular

2 Episodic

3 Linear.

Circular

This refers to a film that actually begins at the end of the story. Although this sounds a bit strange, surprisingly there are many films that start at the end and then use a series of **flashbacks** to tell the story. Sometimes the film is one long flashback and returns to the beginning at the end. One such film is *Titanic* (1997). This starts with the exploration of the wreck of the Titanic before introducing us to the character of Rose as an old lady. We then flashback to the main narrative through her memories, only returning to the present almost at the end of the film. The narrative then emotionally concludes with the re-uniting of Rose and Jack, when Rose dies.

Key terms

Flashback: When we see a scene from the past that is somehow relevant to the narrative in the present.

Voice-over: When a character from the film or an unknown voice gives us additional information over the top of the action of the film.

Close up: the classroom

- Can you think of 3 different films with circular narrative structures?
- How does the structure aid your understanding of the film?
- Does the circular structure tell you anything important about the characters?
- Do you think the structure had any impact on your enjoyment of the narrative?

Episodic

Not every narrative with flashbacks and voice-overs is a circular narrative. Unsurprisingly the episodic structure is used in a number of Superhero films, as they often involve narratives based on comic books or graphic novels. Superhero films can be made up of different stories stitched together so the defined episodes are often really noticeable. The film *Watchmen*, for example, follows the stories of different but linked characters relatively separately from each other to reflect the 12 instalments of the original graphic novel. *The Dark Knight* separates into a number of different stories with identifiable endings; some of these stories are completed within the film's narrative, but the ending of the film is left slightly open to allow for further exploration of the *wider* narrative about the ambiguous role of a Superhero who operates outside, but in co-operation with, traditional institutions of law and order – the police and politicians.

Such a structure can be compared to the way novels break up a story into chapters. Sometimes chapters follow on directly in sequence, but sometimes different aspects of the story are introduced that (deliberately) interrupt or disrupt the chronology of the narrative.

Close up: the classroom

Experiment with changing the narrative structure of a well-known story from linear to circular and then episodic – try a fairy story or a well-known film narrative.

- You will probably find it more difficult to create an episodic narrative – but maybe this suits some stories more than others?

- Share your ideas with the class and see which stories were most successful.

Linear

A linear narrative is the most commonly used narrative structure in mainstream film and other media, and is the easiest to follow. It refers to a story that is told from start to end in the order in which events happen. We sometimes describe these as 'cause and effect' narratives, in so far as the consequences of one event usually have an effect on something else and things move along in this way until the narrative is resolved.

34: *The Orphanage*

This is not to say that linear narratives are by definition predictable, as there can be many twists and turns and audiences may still have to work hard to discover what's going on. *Twilight – Eclipse* (2010) and *The Orphanage* (2007) are good examples of recent films with intriguing and complicated plots and linear structures.

Narrative viewpoint

Films lead us into reading narratives in a particular way using various techniques. A voice-over narration may imply which characters we are meant to feel most connected to, and the choices made in terms of camera shots can reinforce this by showing us events from their point of view. To make us really feel part of the film's narrative, a director can use a **restricted narrative** viewpoint in which we the audience only get to know as much as the on-screen characters do. Therefore, we are just as puzzled as the characters are, and have to work out what is going to happen as the story goes along just as they do. Crime films often use a restricted narrative because working out the clues alongside the detective is part of the enjoyment of the genre.

> **Key terms**
>
> **Restricted narrative:** A narrative where we know only as much as the characters in the film.
>
> **Omniscient narrative:** Where the audience knows more than the characters about narrative events and plot details.

Close up: the classroom

Compare the narrative viewpoints in *X-Men 2* and *Spider-Man*.

- Which of these is restricted and which omniscient?
- How do you know this?
- Why is this important to the way the story unfolds in each film?
- How does this viewpoint add to your enjoyment of the films?

Often, though, films give us a 'god-like' overview of the narrative, where we are aware of much more than the main characters. The audience both sees events that the main characters can't or don't, and are made aware of the potential consequences of those events, which builds suspense and tension. This is defined as an **omniscient narrative**. Disaster films are a good example of this as the audience is given clues to the oncoming disaster and are privy to the scientist's knowledge before those in authority choose to act.

Narrative time and space

When we watch a film we are aware of the beginning and end of a story – but it is important to consider that the beginning of a film's narrative is not necessarily the start of a character's story; unless they were born at the beginning of the film – which is true of some films. Consequently the ending of the film is not the end of everything –even *2012* (2009) when the world ends is not really the end of the world!

A film does not give absolutely every detail of a character's life as it would be pretty boring to watch a character asleep or brushing their teeth all the time.

Time is manipulated quite a lot in films without us really thinking about it. It can be stretched to allow a moment to last longer than it would in real life and it can be reduced so all the uninteresting or irrelevant parts of a character's day are cut.

Close up: the classroom

In *The Lion King* Simba grows from a cub to an adolescent lion within the film and in *Notting Hill* (1999) a year is shown to go past apparently in one shot. This is shown through a clever manipulation of narrative time.

Have a look at key extracts from the films and analyse how and why this manipulation takes place.

A film is just a part of a bigger story really, a story about an important event in a person's life, or in a particular galaxy. But within these narratives, time is manipulated and the story is usually condensed to give us a coherent film with a beginning, middle and end.

Editing plays a big part in how this happens and is very important to manipulating narrative time so that we understand the narrative.

We accept the gaps in narrative time created during the editing process – referred to as **ellipsis** – as it is just part of what makes a film a film and not real life; this is similar to how we accept the addition of music to create mood.

Parallel editing allows us to see two or more events at the same time and this therefore links these events together. This often happens to create drama – something is happening that we can see but not everyone within the narrative of the film can see it.

When a film runs in real time, this is generally used to give a sense of realism or maybe to create tension.

Key terms

Ellipsis: Events that are missed out of a narrative as they are not needed for plot development.

Parallel editing: Cuts that are designed to show us different events that are going on at the same time within a narrative.

Close up: the classroom

Film a one minute sequence of different things in your classroom and around school, including a conversation and someone walking or running in different places. Use different camera shots. Then experiment with editing to manipulate time and to create different moods by changing the pace. You will be surprised how editing can really change a narrative.

Narrative theory

Some writers have looked at narratives and applied various theories to the typical ways they work. Applying theories to your studies can sometimes restrict your thinking but on other occasions it can be quite useful in looking for patterns within genres or narratives.

The 3-Act Structure

According to Syd Field, author of *Screenplay* and *The Screen Writer's Workbook*, most screenplays follow a 3-act structure which consists of Set-up, Confrontation and Resolution. This developed from an earlier theory by the Bulgarian, Tzvetan Todorov, who applied a 5-act structure to literature.

Act 1 establishes the background to the story, introduces the characters, gives us any back-story we need to know and introduces the main plot. It can be referred to as the 'equilibrium' where everything in life is normal and in 'balance'.

Act 2 is where the main action takes place, also referred to as the disruption to the equilibrium in an earlier version of this theory.

Act 3 is the resolution, where all the loose ends of the plot are tied together and some sort of ending occurs. Often this ending leaves audiences satisfied but sometimes we are left with some unresolved issues so a sequel can follow!

Character types

It is also interesting to consider when films use typical characters and if, by comparing films, you can identify the types of characters used in particular genres. For example, we find it easy to talk about heroes and villains in lots of different film genres and these are clearly identifiable character types. In some films there is often a love interest and if the hero is a man there may be a woman who needs saving – a character type that is described as the 'princess'. You should not presume the 'princess' has to be a woman. In modern terms the 'princess' could refer to a character who needs 'rescuing' or is the 'reward' and this is not always a woman in contemporary narratives. Lara Croft is a good example of a modern day hero who does the rescuing rather than being rescued herself.

Other characters that have been identified are:

- the false hero – who pretends they are going to help the hero
- the helper – works alongside the hero
- the donor – gives something useful to the hero
- the dispatcher – sends the hero on his or her mission.

These ideas were originally developed nearly 100 years ago by Vladimir Propp in relation to Russian folk stories, so it does not relate directly to films and is quite simplistic. But it is interesting to consider how Propp's character types can be applied to many modern film narratives. Many Superhero films are likely to conform to these types because of the nature of the comic book or graphic novel approach to character and the kinds of themes these narratives cover. Also, don't imagine all Superhero films have male heroes and weak women!

35: Elektra – no weak woman (*Elektra*, 2005)

Close up: the classroom

Think of 3 different films you have seen from different genres and try to apply Propp's character types to the films.

- Do most films have these character types?
- What does this suggest?

Chapter 7 Representation

In this section we will cover:

- How people and places are represented in different genres.
- How audiences read representations of people and places differently.
- How films construct ideas in a certain way to get across certain messages.

What is representation

Representation is a key concept in Film and Media Studies as it refers to how the world is re-presented to us in the media. It is important for *everyone* to consider representation, not just students, as so much of how we understand the world today is seen through the 'eyes' of the media. Think about how you tend to discuss celebrities and film stars with your friends. Who are your favourites and why? Much of what you like about them will be things you have found out in the media and therefore not necessarily the truth.

Our points of view about things are usually formed by a number of different factors: parents, friends, our cultural background and the media. What we read, what we see and other people's opinions that we value shape the way we view and understand the world. When we watch a film, it is important to remember that the images shown of a place or a person are selected in order to communicate meaning and create a particular response from the audience. These representations are evident through choices made within the narrative and also through the choice of stars for certain roles. Film language can also be used to 'say' things about people and places .

Close up: the classroom

Watch the first half of *Transformers* (2007).

- Straight away we are being introduced to particular character types: the tough soldier, the schoolboy geek, the sexy girl.

- These characters have particular functions within the narrative and clearly represent the types of people that the audience will be able to identify with or recognise.

- Why is it important to do this in a film?

How people and groups are represented in film

In Film and Media Studies we tend to talk about the representation of groups and separate people into these groups according to ethnicity, different abilities, age, gender, nationality, region, religion, sexuality and social class. This can lead to stereotyping, which we will discuss shortly, but it is useful to be able to consider how groups are represented in film and if these representations match our experiences or views.

Sometimes a film will purposefully challenge our viewpoints of certain groups or offer us new ways of considering age or gender perhaps. The animated film *Up* (2009), for example, offers an amusing and interesting representation of old age, as the hero is an old man. In some ways the main character is clearly a stereotypical old man. He is grumpy, has false teeth and has to use a walking stick. However, he is a hero, has to fight a villain (also an old man – even older than him!) and he goes on an adventure.

People usually belong to a number of groups. We are all a certain age and belong to a certain country but we may not particularly see ourselves as representations of 'youth' or 'Britishness'. How would you describe these two groups?

Some film genres often use stereotypical representations. Action films and Superhero films often have stereotypical, masculine heroes, for example, possibly because the characterisation is not as important to these genres as spectacle and action.

Close up: the classroom

- In pairs pick two heroes from Superhero films. Name the heroes and then list their stereotypical characteristics.

- Are either of the heroes different in any way from the stereotypical Superhero? Note down the differences.

Stereotyping

Let's be honest – we are all guilty of making assumptions about people from time to time. It may be because of where they are from (be it a different part of town or a foreign country), what they look like, or what religion they practise. When representations are over-simplistic and repeated in media forms, this is described as **stereotyping**. Sometimes the media reinforces, or influences, some of our prejudices or beliefs through representations in the news, in films, computer games and on television. Advertisements often use stereotypical representations, to get messages across quickly and simply: 'the lad' in beer commercials and the sexy woman in perfume advertisements. But sometimes stereotypes can be offensive and hurtful so it is important that we recognise stereotypes and consider alternative representations. This will become more apparent as you study films from other cultures.

Archetypes

Some representations are passed down through myths, legends and folk tales and these are referred to as **archetypes**. You may have heard a character referred to as an *archetypal villain*, suggesting there is something about them that makes them instantly recognisable as an evil character by a particular culture or society. Darth Vader and Lex Luthor are good examples of archetypal villains in film – but why?

36: Archvillains: Darth Vader and Lex Luthor

Is it obvious these two are villains just from these images?

When studying Superhero films you will be introduced to clearly defined heroes and villains. Often the villain will have physical deformities and may have been driven insane because of them – consider The Joker for example. Often ugliness is seen as a punishment for being bad! Heroes are nearly always strong and attractive, so what message does this give us – that anyone who isn't beautiful is bad? Not all Superhero films are quite so simplistic, though – *Watchmen*, for example, has quite complex characters and some dark, violent scenes, so it will be interesting to compare the different styles of Superhero films.

Close up: the classroom

- Visit the website http://tamicowden.com/villains.htm and create a poster explaining and illustrating famous heroes and villains.

Society and beliefs change throughout time and how people live in many places in the world is very different from how it was 50 years ago. This is why representations within the media change. Think about the representation of Native Americans in the Hollywood westerns of the late 1940s and early 1950s (who at that time were called 'Red Indians'). Why do you think these representations have changed during the past 50 years? What is suggested by the different ways Native Americans are described?

Certain genres often contain characters that are only associated with that type of film. We come to expect these characters; they seem to 'fit' the style of the film and we can easily predict what their role will be within the narrative. These representations are referred to as **generic types**.

Key terms

Generic type: A certain personality or type of person seen repeatedly in a particular genre.

37: Bruce Willis: arrogant, tough and fearless?

38: Robert Pattinson: sensitive strong and fearless?

Close up: the classroom

These two well-known stars seem to be representing generic types in these images.

- How would you describe each 'type'?

- What genre of film would you see these characters in?

- Do you think these characters are stereotypes in any way?

- Can you think of other characters in other films that compare well to these three?

By now you should be making links between genre, narrative and representation. Genre changes over time; not just because of technology or film-makers, but because society changes and so, too, do people's views.

Ideology

The study of representation in films is also concerned with who made the film and where it was made. Every society has its own **ideology**, which means its own values and beliefs, which will be evident in a country's laws, within its culture and within the media. That is not to say that a film-maker will consciously *only* make films that support the ideology of the country of their birth or in which they are working – in fact, sometimes entirely the opposite is true; they will not always support everything their government or the media says. But films made in different countries often have an identifiable 'look' that can implicitly reflect the values, beliefs and ideas that are common within that country because those same values, beliefs and ideas have shaped the film-makers who have made the film and the institutions that supported its production.

The film *Amélie* for example, clearly shows a particular viewpoint of France and French life. The music, the colours, the attitudes of characters all reflect aspects of 'Frenchness' that are part of the enjoyment of the film for audiences. Of course, not all French films will show France, or even Paris, in the same way – one dramatic alternative example being *La Haine* (1995) – but this is not to say either of these films is representing aspects of French life inaccurately.

> **Key terms**
>
> **Ideology:** This refers to a group's, an individual's or a country's values.

left: 39: *Four Weddings and a Funeral* (1994)

right: 40: *This is England* (2006)

Close up: the classroom

These are stills from two very well-known British films.

- What aspects of British culture do they show? Do you think they show any aspects of 'British ideology'?

It is interesting that most cinema audiences in Britain watch films made in Hollywood, so nearly all the films we watch carry American ideological values.

Realism is an important concept which relates to representation but it is also quite difficult to define. In essence, film is a realist medium. Whether we are whisked to another universe or an inner city estate in Manchester a film-maker will want to make the narrative and the characters within that setting believable. The techniques used by the film-maker – camera work, music and editing – combine to involve us so much in the action of the film that we allow ourselves to forget that time and space and our emotions are being manipulated.

Social realist films are a conscious attempt to reject stereotypical representations because this is a genre where character complexity and delivering a message are very important. It is by working against conventional media representations – in film, but also in the press and on TV – that these films can make points about our society and its assumptions. *Yasmin* (2004) is a good example of a social realist film.

41: *Yasmin* (2004)

Key terms

Realism: A believable representation of events.

Social realism: A style of film-making that deals with social issues and uses particular filmic techniques.

Close up: the classroom

Watch the opening of *Yasmin*.

How does this differ from Hollywood films you have seen in terms of:

- Setting
- Characters
- Style
- Narrative.

The audience and 'readings'

Every individual's response to a film is unique. Yours may be linked to many issues, from your social and cultural background but also your own tastes and viewpoints, which aren't necessarily those of your friends and family, even if you are part of the same social and cultural groups. So when studying representation, you also need to consider the importance of the audience, the viewer of the film – you. Remember that your opinion of a film, or the messages you receive from it, will not be the same as everyone else's. In Film Studies we call a response to a film a 'reading' and, depending on the factors described above, this can be a **preferred**, **negotiated** or **oppositional reading**.

If you agree with the majority viewpoint of the audience, or understand and accept the points the film-maker is getting across, you have a preferred reading of the film's intentions (overt or implicit). But, of course, film-makers do not always make their intentions explicit or may even *prefer* their film to be 'read' on different levels, so this isn't always so obvious. If you agree with *some* of the film's representations and appreciate *some* of the points made, but not others, then this is a negotiated reading. And if you really dislike a film and everything it stands for, yours will be an oppositional reading of the film.

Key terms

Preferred reading:
When your reading of the film is what the director was intending.

Negotiated reading:
When you read some of the ideas that are intended but do not see or agree with others.

Oppositional reading:
When you disagree with the film's messages and values.

Close up: the exam

Representation is particularly significant to your studies on films made outside Hollywood. In this exam, you will be asked to consider how people and places are represented in the films you have watched. Here is a chance to practise the kinds of things you will be asked to do in the exam on one of the set films.

In your study of representation you should consider what kinds of characters appear in a film and what narrative function they serve.

Representation is a complex issue and an emotive one, often causing many debates in the classroom. It draws on our experiences of the world and our viewpoints on how we want the world to be. It is always important to think about the choices film-makers have made and what they want us to take away from their films.

What have we learnt?

In this chapter we have seen that when you are studying representation there are many different aspects to consider such as:

- Everything we see or hear on the cinema screen has been constructed to encourage us to read a film in a certain way.

- Film-makers may use 'types' so that we can get to know the characters and their situations quickly.

- We all watch films slightly differently but most of us 'identify' with one or more characters, hoping they 'succeed' in the story.

Chapter 8 Genre Study

In this section we will cover:

- What do we mean by 'genre' in Film Studies?
- How can we identify a film's genre?
- The importance of genre in terms of film institutions and audiences.
- The conventions associated with particular genres.
- The cross-generic nature of particular films.

Introduction

This chapter will show how an understanding of genre can help you to study specific groups of films. It is important to realise that the aim is not simply to identify every film as belonging to a specific genre, but to look at the differences and similarities between films, consider how and why genres change over time, and to understand the ways in which genre is used by industry and audiences.

The word 'genre' refers to a type or category. In your study of books or plays for English, you probably will have encountered the concept of genre. Often the music you listen to or the games you play on your computer or PlayStation are influenced by the kinds of genres that you enjoy.

Genre can be important when choosing which film you want to watch at home, or in the cinema. If it influences an audience's choice of film then it will affect the kinds of films that are produced. Film producers have to be sure that there is a healthy market for their films if they want to survive in a very competitive market.

Genre study has become a key way of looking at how films are made, analysed and received by audiences. There is a massive number of films which could be studied so it is helpful to be able to break down the list into groups and consider them in smaller chunks. If we do this, we can see what they have in common, how they differ, and what film language they share with themselves and films in general. This helps us to understand the films themselves, the meanings that are created and the reason for any genre's continued use or popularity .

Close up: the classroom

Write down the title of a film you have seen recently.

- In pairs, share your choice and decide which genre you think it might belong to.

- Note down the features that helped you to recognise the film's genre. Was it always easy to spot the genre? If not, why not?

Often you can recognise the genre of a film very quickly. It may be the setting, characters or the themes that help you recognise the genre, or you may have spotted typical plots or props.

Because the film industry is so important in our world today, and because so many films have been made since the industry began well over a hundred years ago, it would be very difficult to study film without breaking them down into groups and thinking about them in terms of differences and similarities. It isn't just films that are studied this way. If you think about your typical school day, teaching is divided into subject areas and then each subject is tackled in terms of specific topics. So the study of genre can help us to see what certain films have in common, how they differ and how film language is used to communicate particular themes and issues. It also allows a consideration of the ways in which genre is used and the reasons for its continued use and popularity.

How we identify genre

Genre categories are broad enough to accommodate practically any film ever made, although film categories can never be precise. Most films belong to at least one major genre, but they can also contain elements of other genres. What, though, makes a group of films a 'genre'? In simple terms, it's the things they have in common.

As we've already said, when we watch a film we can often identify its genre fairly quickly. That means we recognise features, patterns and film techniques which are common to several films – they become typical of that group of films. So in a particular genre, you often see typical:

- settings (where and when a film is set)
- characters
- narratives and plots
- themes or issues
- props or significant objects
- style.

These typical features are called **conventions**.

Identifying genre through conventional themes and issues

A problem is that no genre can be defined in a single hard and fast way. Some genres stand out by their subjects – the **themes** and **issues** they deal with. For example, a gangster film usually centres on large-scale urban crime.

Close up: the classroom

- What themes or issues are important in the following genres?
  - science fiction
  - horror
  - Western.
- Share your ideas with the rest of the class.

You have probably agreed that in terms of themes or issues, a science fiction film usually deals with the effect of science upon society or individual characters. When considering the horror film you may have encountered difficulties because there are so many horror sub-genres – genres within genres – like the gothic horror or the 'slasher' movie. However, we can say that horror films usually deal with people's worst nightmares – their fears and particularly their fear of the unknown. The Western often portrays how desolate and hard life was for American frontier families. This may be shown through conflict between settlers and Native Americans, or between the US Cavalry defending the interests of settlers against the Native Americans. The other major Western genre conflict is between small communities and their struggle to uphold the rule of law against outlaws.

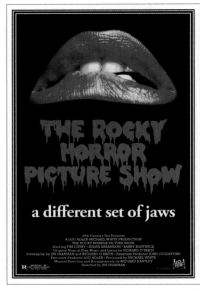

42: *The Rocky Horror Picture Show* (1975) & 43: *Mars Attacks!* (1996)

Close up: the classroom

- Look carefully at the two film posters opposite. To which genres do the films being advertised belong?

- Which other genre conventions are evident in the posters?

Other ways of identifying genre

You may realise that you can identify a film's genre through stylistic or visual conventions. So themes and issues are not the only way of identifying genres. For example, musicals are recognised mainly by their style – the way in which they include singing or dancing or both. The detective film is partly defined by its plot, which involves an investigation and the solution of a mystery. That is also true of the biographical film (a 'biopic'). We expect a biopic to trace the main character's entire life. In other cases, like the cop thriller, it's the characters who are the obvious convention: the shifty informer, the comic sidekick, the impatient captain who despairs of getting the squad detectives to follow procedures.

Other genre conventions are based on **film techniques**. Sombre, low key lighting is used in the horror film and the thriller. The action picture often relies on rapid cutting and slow-motion violence. In a melodrama, an emotional twist may be underscored by a sudden burst of sad music.

Close up: the classroom

Watch the opening sequence of either *Batman Begins* (2005) or *Hellboy* (2004).

- How many different genres are signalled?

- What themes are introduced?

- What film techniques are used?

- Are there any conventional characters? How did you identify them?

As a visual medium, cinema can also define genres through conventional **iconography**. A genre's iconography consists of recurring symbolic images that carry meaning from film to film. Objects and settings often furnish iconography for a genre. A close-up of a gravestone in a dark, storm-swept cemetery would probably be enough to identify a film as a horror (although the opening of *Hellboy* demonstrates that the iconography associated with one genre can easily be used within another). A war film takes place in a battle-scarred landscape; the science fiction film is often set in the future or on starships and on distant planets. Even actors can become iconographic, for example, Tom Cruise in the action thriller, Jennifer Aniston in the romantic comedy.

Apart from style and iconography, you can say that some genres are defined mainly by the distinctive **emotional effect** they aim for, such as amusement in comedy, tension in the thriller or, as we've already seen, fear in the horror film.

Genre mixing

Key terms

Hybrid film: Where conventions from two different genres are put together in the film.

Genre mixing is common throughout popular film-making. We can have musical Westerns (*Calamity Jane* (1953)), musical melodramas (*A Star Is Born* (1976)), and a musical horror movie (*The Rocky Horror Picture Show* (1975)). *Mars Attacks!* (1996) combines science fiction with comedy. *Alien* merges the horror film, science fiction and the thriller. *Shaun of the Dead* mixes comedy with the zombie movie. Films which mix genres are called hybrid. The fact that genres can intermingle does not, however, mean that there are no distinctions among them. Perhaps the best way to identify a genre is to recognise how audiences and film-makers, at different historical periods and in different places, have distinguished one sort of movie from another.

By knowing conventions, the viewer has a pathway into the film. This knowledge allows the genre movie to communicate information quickly and economically. When we see a young gangster we strongly suspect that ultimately he will be made to pay for his mistakes. Alternatively, a film can revise or reject the conventions associated with a certain genre. For example, *Life is Beautiful* is an Italian comedy largely set in a Nazi concentration camp during the Second World War. Film-makers may seek to surprise or shock viewers by breaking their expectations that a certain convention will be followed. Audiences expect the genre film to offer something familiar, but they also demand fresh variations on it. The film-maker may devise something just slightly, or even markedly, different, but it will still be based on familiar genre conventions. The tension between similarity and difference is central to genre films.

Perhaps, then, a genre is best thought of as a rough category whose main conventions are shared by both audience and film-maker.

Genre, Industry and Audience

We've thought about the ways in which audiences use genre. For example, it allows us:

- to compare one film with another

- to choose which film we want to go and see at the cinema

- to 'read' important narrative clues quickly and effectively

- to predict what might happen to particular characters.

Can you think of any other ways in which audiences use genre?

But what about the film industry? Genre categorisation is equally important to film producers. They use genre as a simple yet powerful way of selling their films to a specific target audience. If they know a particular genre is popular with audiences, they will feel confident in investing money in it. In other words, it limits the financial risk they have to take.

Nevertheless, genres have to maintain their freshness and appeal. We may love a particular genre but we certainly don't want to see exactly the same film over and over again. Producers are constantly looking for ways of refreshing an old genre. For example, horror films have been popular at various times throughout the history of film, *Nosferatu* (1922) terrified audiences during the silent film era, Universal's *Frankenstein* (1931) shocked in the 1930s, Hammer's *Dracula* (1958) and its sequels thrilled in the 1960s, *Scream* (1996) added a new ironic dimension to the slasher film in the 1990s and *Twilight* (2008) appealed to a teenage audience in the noughties. Clearly, this genre is constantly changing and adapting to new audience demands, and innovative film-makers will want to put their own stamp on it. This is how genres evolve and change.

44: The changing face of vampires: 21st century and the 1960s '– *Twilight* (2008) and *Dracula* (1958)

When you begin your preparation for Paper 1: Exploring Film, you will spend a significant amount of time focusing on one particular genre – the Superhero movie. You will need to explore this genre in depth. You'll be focusing on:

- how the conventions of the genre are used
- how they combine repetition and variation of those familiar conventions and
- how they might mix in conventions from other genres.

You'll then start to recognise how genres reflect the times in which they were made and how they can be used to raise issues.

You'll also have the chance to explore the use of genre creatively through pre-production and production tasks. This will give you the opportunity to explore films as both audience and film-maker, and to recognise the meanings that are created.

What have we learnt?

In this chapter we have learnt:

- that genres are constantly changing and adapting
- that many films are hybrids
- that some films are easier to categorise than others
- that genres are important in terms of audience expectation and reducing the risk of financial failure for producers.

Part 2 Exploring Film

In this part you will learn:

- Film Language. How a mainstream Hollywood genre uses both micro and macro elements to create meaning and achieve its aims.

- Film Organisations. You will explore the modern Hollywood system and how it manages production, distribution and exhibition in order to 'sell' its product.

- Audience. What is an audience? Who is an audience? How do producers find an audience? How and why do we consume the films we do?

1: Superheroes – who *are* these people? (Clockwise from top left: *Spider-Man 2*, *Iron Man*, *Sin City*, *The Dark Knight*)

Chapter 1 The Superhero Movie – An Introduction

In this chapter we will cover:

- Defining the Superhero and the Superhero movie.

Introduction

Key terms

Film Language: The techniques used to create meaning in films.

Film Industry: The commercial aspect of making films – production, distribution and exhibition.

In this part of the course you will focus on one specific Hollywood genre – the Superhero movie. This will involve three main areas of study – **film language**, **film organisations** (**the film industry**) and **film audiences**. You will use the tools you have learned in the film language part of the course to explore this genre to increase your understanding of its boundaries and the films that fall within them. As well as this you will look at how the Superhero movie is a product, including how and why Hollywood continues to revisit the genre for financial reasons and what all this means for audiences.

Superheroes and the Superhero Genre

So what might be the defining characteristic of a genre called 'the Superhero movie'? Is it a film based on a comic book Superhero character? Well, it has to be wider than that as not all movie Superheroes started their lives in comic books. Is it just a film that features a Superhero or Superheroes? Perhaps the first question we need to ask is – what actually *is* a Superhero?

Is it somebody with superpowers? Not necessarily, as Batman does not actually have any super (or meta-human) powers. It is more about what the character chooses to do with the powers they have. If they choose to 'suit-up' and defend the weak, truth, justice and any number of other laudable aims, then we may be getting closer. This is described quite succinctly in *Superheroes! Capes and Crusaders In Comics And Films*, by Roz Kaveney:

> A superhero... is a man or woman with powers that are either massive extensions of human strengths and capabilities, or fundamentally different in kind, which he or she uses to fight for truth, justice and the protection of the innocent. A substantial minority of people without powers as such share a commitment to the superhero mission, so they are generally regarded as superheroes in spite of the absence of such powers.

If that's what a Superhero is, what's a Superhero movie? Here's my definition:

A Superhero movie centres on individuals who use their powers for public rather than personal good, often against an enemy who uses their powers for personal rather than public good. Most are sourced from comic books.

Perhaps Ben Parker (Spider-Man's uncle) said it even better:

'With great power comes great responsibility.'

The details implied by these definitions will be considered in chapters two–five.

More on...

Comic books, their main publishers (DC Comics and Marvel) and how they are turned into movies at www.wjec.co.uk-filmstudies-gcse

Close up: the classroom

- List as many Superhero movies as you can think of. Compile a class list.

- What features do you think they share?

- Compile your first list of Superhero movie features.

Chapter 2 Identifying The Genre – Codes And Conventions

In this chapter we will cover:

- The Superhero movie in more detail.
- The codes and conventions of the Superhero movie.
- Audience expectations.

Close up: the exam

Whenever you watch something that is labelled as a specific genre, try to think about what puts it in that group. Is the label right or wrong? What characteristics does it have?

Key terms

Codes and Conventions: The detailed 'rules' of the genre. The micro and macro aspects we come to expect when we hear a genre name.

What Do We Expect From The Superhero Movie?

All genres have a 'menu' of things that the audience expects to see played out in a film of that kind. A list of these things can be referred to as the genre's **codes and conventions**. This list will always incorporate a degree of flexibility. Some films may not include them all and some films may use them in very different ways. Yet if the film is to meet our expectations of the genre then some of these features must be present.

Close up: the classroom

What are the ingredients a film needs to be called a Superhero movie? Make your own list of codes and conventions.

- As a group or class try to agree on a basic list of ingredients for a Superhero movie. Refer to films you have seen to help with your decision.
- Keep a note of your list. Check films against it to test both the film and the list.

As set out in Part 1 of this book, Film Language, here are the kinds of things we typically look for in identifying any genre:

1. **Setting:** what is its location or historical time period?
2. **Themes:** what ideas, concepts and/or emotions does it deal with?

3. **Characters:** powers, secret identity, stereotypes and archetypes.

4. **Props or significant objects:** the small things or details we expect.

5. **Narrative and plot:** typical kinds of stories that are told.

6. **Style:** fights and destruction, the look of the film, editing, shots, cinematography.

Close up: the classroom

Look at the list above and see how many examples you can think of from Superhero movies.

- Choose a Superhero movie and apply the list to it specifically.
- How many typical codes and conventions does it have?
- What important features does it have that do not typically feature on the list?

If you tried the activity, now compare it to what I came up with, below. How did I do?

1. Setting

2: New York City – well served by Superheroes

Typically this would be an American city, often un-named. Most Superheroes ply their trade on the seamier side of urban America where their main protagonist, the criminal, can be found. In a lot of cases, this city is New York (e.g. Spider-Man) or a re-named New York (e.g. Metropolis). It can even be a transplanted dark side of New York (e.g. Gotham City).

Additionally, a Superhero's job will often involve saving the world, so locations often go global as in *The Fantastic Four* (2005) or even intergalactic as in *The Green Lantern* (2011).

On a smaller scale, it is about dark alleys and dangerous places – Superheroes sometimes protecting specific neighbourhoods such as

Hell's Kitchen in *Daredevil* (2003). Additionally, it will also involve a headquarters, either secret (X-Men's Xavier's school for the gifted) or public (The Fantastic Four's Baxter Building).

The time period is almost exclusively contemporary, except when an 'origin' story looks back over a longer period of time, as with Captain America in the 1940s.

2. Themes

The themes that are common to the Superhero movie can be divided into 'the public', the visible struggles of the hero, and 'the private', the personal struggles of the hero.

The 'public'

These themes include the big areas of moral debate, good versus evil, what's right and what's wrong. These can be simply personified in the **oppositional** figures of the hero and the villain. In films like *Superman* and *Spider-Man*, it is fairly obvious who is acting for good and who is acting for evil. In other examples, this is not always so clear and our heroes are faced with moral dilemmas that are not quite so black and white. In the *Batman* films, the pursuit of 'natural justice' and the clash of vigilantism and the rule of law, sometimes compromised by corruption, make for a very murky mix.

Other broader themes can also be present, such as issues of race, gender, sexuality, disability, class, the environment, rich and poor, science or politics. We will consider some of these in more detail in chapter 4.

The 'private'

On a smaller scale, many more personal themes are dealt with repeatedly in the Superhero movie, notably the hero's relationships and responsibilities and how these are affected by their powers and 'mission'. The wrestling with their conscience and the sacrifice this often leads to is fertile ground for the writers looking for character development. A hero is often faced with moral dilemmas when making decisions about their public persona that will inevitably impact on their private one. Their motivations are also often questioned by both themselves and the villain in this wrestling with the morality of their situation. Overall, our heroes tend to place their private needs below their public responsibilities, whereas a villain is often defined as one who reverses these priorities.

3. Characters

There are certain characters we expect to see or recognise in the Superhero movie, the most obvious of these being a clear hero and a

Key terms

Oppositions: Where characters personify two aspects of the same idea, or two 'sides of the same coin', e.g. predator and prey.

clear villain. These are often classic examples of the **binary opposite** – in Batman and the Joker we have very different characters, two opposite sides of the concept of control or power. Batman is dour, deliberate, disciplined, trained and calculating to the point of (some say beyond) paranoia. In contrast, The Joker is exactly that – darkly comedic, anarchistic, attention-seeking and just the wrong side of insane. Yet what makes their 'relationship' interesting is that the Joker can plan and scheme just as well as Batman, a quality they mutually respect.

Alongside these main protagonists are the supporting characters, in some ways '**stock characters**' we often expect to see:the sidekick (Iron Man and Rhodey), a love interest (The Hulk and Betty Ross), family (Aunt May, the Kents) and/or supporters (Alfred Pennyworth, Lucius Fox and Commissioner Gordon).

4. Props or significant objects

Like all genres, there are certain props or objects that remind us we are watching a Superhero movie. The most obvious one of these has to be the costume. It can serve to protect a secret identity (Spider-Man), be the source of the character's powers (Iron Man, Venom) or be a means of identification like a normal uniform (X-Men). Gadgets and weapons are important as well. Batman relies on his 'hi-tech toys' as supplied by Lucius Fox. Vehicles are also often identified with Superhero movies. Will a Wonder Woman film ever be complete without her invisible plane? A **Macguffin** is sometimes a vital part of the narrative as the hero must beat the villain to securing this vital world-threatening object. In all Superhero movies, there will be personal objects – the small things or details we have come to expect.

5. Narrative and plot

In many ways the narrative of the Superhero movie could be described as its most limited aspect, 'good versus evil' being a fair summary of a lot of them. But within this simplicity – more simple even than a **high concept pitch?** – many different stories can be told.

Most first films in a Superhero franchise will be an 'origin' story, detailing for a wider audience how they acquired their powers and became a Superhero. For example *The Fantastic Four* tells the story of how exposure to a 'mutagenic storm' 'gifts' the main protagonists their superpowers and the 'narrative fallout' that results.

Typical subsequent narratives will concern a loss of powers and/or belief in their cause. In *Superman II* and *Spider-Man 2*, both heroes have to deal with spells without their powers.

Key terms

Binary opposite: A conflict between two opposing ideas or characters, at the root of most popular narratives. This conflict is generally resolved at the end of the narrative.

Key terms

Stock Characters and Stereotypes: Simple characters that are only very superficial and depend on our knowledge of clichés to recognise them.

Key terms

Macguffin: An object, the securing of which drives the narrative forward.

The object around which the plot revolves, but, as to what that object *specifically* is, 'the audience don't care' (Alfred Hitchcock, who coined the term).

High concept pitch: A pitch for a film based on a very basic narrative idea. They will often rely on special effects and stars to make the concept work.

The narrative instigated by the villains will usually involve revenge upon the hero. For example, there is Harry Osborn (The Green Goblin Mark 2) in *Spider-Man 3* (2007); or there are the audacious crimes that range all the way up to global conquest such as Dr. Doom's plan in *Fantastic Four: Rise Of The Silver Surfer* (2007). Other common sub-plots can involve romantic entanglements and the foreshadowing of future storylines for possible sequels.

Close up: creative work

Try to think of some Superhero movies or blockbuster films and what their high concept pitch may have been.

- Write out the brief pitch for 3 or 4 of the films on your list.
- Try to come up with a high concept for a new Superhero movie.
- Write a pitch for it.

6. Style

This can encompass many different aspects that add up to the look and feel of the film, including editing and cinematography (in particular, specific camera shots). In the Superhero movie, many elements of style conform to what we would expect from an action movie – a quick overall pace, with some slower moments to provide contrast or 'shade' for high explosive action sequences. The Superhero movie has another dimension, however, as its original source material is more visual than most others – the comic book being a storyboard of sorts. So we will often see elements of comic book presentation leaking into the film, whole panels (single comic book pictures) sometimes being transplanted to the screen. For example, when Peter Parker throws away his costume in *Spider-Man 2*, the scene is almost identical to a classic comic book cover depicting the same 'Spider-Man no more' event.

As you study the Superhero genre you may well be able to add further features and examples to this brief rundown that is intended to give you a grasp of the major features.

Close up: the classroom

Look at the list of ingredients for a Superhero movie you made for the first activity in this section. Does it need amending?

- Make any changes you think are needed. Try to explain any additions or subtractions from your list.

Close up: the exam

When dealing with codes and conventions concentrate on the ones that feature most heavily in the film you are discussing. Remember to ask questions yourself, like are the codes and conventions being used in a normal way or is there something unusual going on?

What have we learnt?

- The codes and conventions of the Superhero movie are relatively simple and straightforward.

- This chapter has focused on the most common, the foundations of the genre if you like. The basics remain fairly constant – we have a Superhero, we have a super villain and a mission to save a girl, the public, a city or even the whole world.

- There are others, sometimes specific to sub-genres, e.g. the comedy Superhero movie. Hopefully you will add to the list yourself as you explore the genre.

3: Odin to Thor: 'No son, we're not gods anymore, we're superheroes now.' Not so much code of honour as genre code (and conventions).

Chapter 3 Iconography

In this chapter we will cover:

- What is iconography?
- What is the iconography of the Superhero movie?
- How is iconography used by the film-maker?

4: *Superman Returns:* The iconography returned, but what about the audience?

What are the key visual features of the Superhero movie?

Iconography in genre films are those images or things that we use on an almost instinctive level to identify where a film 'belongs'. They can also have a hidden meaning that is common across the genre in which they appear. For example, in a genre like the Western we would expect Stetson hats (white = good guy, black = bad guy), cowboys (the individual) wearing them, six guns (power, law), dusty towns, saloons (the 'West'), Monument Valley-style scenery, and so on. In terms of its iconography, the Superhero movie is in some ways very similar, although not as clearly defined through repetition as some of the more established genres.

'Iconic' Objects

There are some objects or things that are iconic and common to most Superhero movies. High on the list must be the 'suit' or costume that often incorporates an instantly recognisable logo. For example, the distinctive red and blue of Superman and the Kryptonian 'S' emblazoned upon his chest.

Most of these costumes follow designs long established in the comic book. It can be a mistake to diverge too much from them. One of the reasons why early attempts to launch The Punisher onto the big screen were not well received was the absence of his unmistakably styled full body skull logo. In other examples, the full or comic book iconic costumes are not used owing to the different visual requirements of film. Director Bryan Singer opted for more subdued X-Men costumes, especially in the case of Wolverine's bright yellow and blue suit, even acknowledging this when Wolverine and Cyclops discuss their uniforms. Cyclops comments: 'Well, what would you prefer? Yellow spandex?'

We would also expect to see other items of equipment and vehicles – gadgets feature highly, especially in the case of Batman. The expensive technology he applies to his war on crime is central to his Superhero persona, even in the 1960s 'comedy' version that features 'shark repellent'. Sophisticated gadgets are not the only iconic equipment belonging to Superheroes. More simple weaponry is also important, like Blade's samurai sword, Daredevil's cane/Billy club and Hellboy's gun, 'The Samaritan'. Sometimes, the suit, the gadget and the weapon combine as in the case of Iron Man's body armour.

The Batmobile is perhaps the most famous vehicle of all but we also have The Fantastic Four's Fantasticar, The X-Men's X-Jet or Blackbird and Ghost Rider's flaming motorcycle. Thankfully we have so far been spared Spider-Man's beach buggy from the 1970s comic book.

Close up: the classroom

- Can you identify the following logos?

- Did you get them all?
- Which ones did you get straight away? Why?
- Which ones did you have to guess or think about? Why?
- Do they all qualify as 'iconic'?
- What does this tell us about iconography?

Places

As we have already established, we expect most Superhero movies to take place in an urban environment. How this environment is used and the parts of it the heroes choose to visit render aspects of it iconic.

At some point, we expect the hero to ascend and look down on the world as a reflection of his heightened powers and his role of protector. Shots of the lone hero perched upon some impressive architectural feature are iconic to both comic book and movie. No *Batman* film would be complete without our hero perched upon a gargoyle somewhere watching over us or pondering his next move. Also familiar is the alleyway where the 'lowlife' can be found: puddles, steam rising, dumpsters, litter and trash of all kinds define this world that the Superhero descends into to fight crime. The Superhero movie also relies on our knowledge of existing iconography, most commonly New York, to give a sense of reality, but at times to symbolise the values the hero is attempting to defend. Is it any coincidence that in *X-Men* (2000), Magneto's evil scheme involves a misuse of the Statue of Liberty?

Imagery

There are many images that have become iconic to the Superhero movie through their repeated use. The development of the hero's powers has become fairly standard and the montage of their experimentation is now well established. Each of these usually culminates with some kind of 'eureka' moment as they finally get to grips with their new skills, be it Spider-Man's webslinging or Iron Man's flying.

These 'testing times' usually occur early on in the film. Towards the end, we would expect to see some form of 'smack-down' fight between the hero and the villain. These are a reflection on film of what would appear as a two-page spread or double splash page in the comics and will often feature high levels of destruction of the combatants' surroundings. In portraying the character, certain 'poses' or 'shapes' have become iconic. For example, Wolverine has his claws crossed menacingly in front of his face, Spider-Man hangs upside down and Superman has his arm outstretched as he flies to a rescue.

Close up: the classroom

Think about some of the Superheroes and their movies you are familiar with and either: Search the internet for iconic pictures of them **Or** draw them in an iconic pose

- For each image briefly explain what you think makes it iconic.

Characters

Without going into too much detail at this stage (as we will be looking at characters and stars later), certain characters are *expected* to be present in a Superhero movie. We might expect to see the Superhero, main villain, a sidekick, a love interest/damsel in distress and a real-world contact or contacts that give the hero perspective and keep them grounded.

Music

Ever since John Williams scored the first *Superman* film in 1978, certain pieces of music have come almost to define the genre. The fanfare style musical cue for the Superhero – rooted in Williams' fanfare for *Superman* – instantly brings the character to mind and has been emulated many times over for both villain and hero alike.

Close up: the exam

Remember, iconography is not just about remembering a list. We need to think *why* things are iconic. Why do they crop up over and over? Are their meanings always the same? Do film-makers change their meanings? Does our changing world sometimes alter the meanings of the icons associated with the Superhero movie?

What have we learnt?

In this chapter we have seen that iconography is about two main things.

- Firstly, the instant recognition factor that the icon in question has.

- Secondly, the meaning that goes with it. It may be a simple reaction like green skin = The Hulk or something with more depth and importance, such as a hero looking down on the city = protector and their power(s).

- It all goes to demonstrate the care that creators exercise in choosing which images to use, how often to use them and the meanings they want them to invoke.

Chapter 4 Style

In this chapter we will cover:

- What do we mean by style?
- What style is the Superhero movie?
- How is film language used to create a style?
- How different or similar is it from other styles of films?

Close up: the exam

When thinking about style it can be useful to think about other genres. How they look and feel different (or the same) from the Superhero movie can help us recognise the style of this genre.

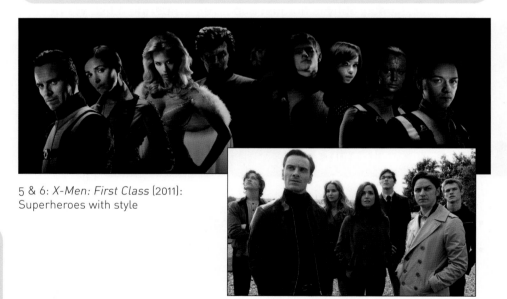

5 & 6: *X-Men: First Class* (2011): Superheroes with style

Key terms

Verisimilitude:
The appearance of reality. The quality of a film that allows the audience to accept it could happen.

The style of the Superhero movie is largely that of classic Hollywood or mainstream cinema. The word often used to describe the abiding quality of this is **verisimilitude**, or 'believability', a film's ability to draw an audience in and make them forget they are in fact only watching a series of scenes on film put together by an editor and director. The 'appearance of reality' is another way to describe it. If we think about most films, it does not take long to come up with real things that happen all the time that never seem to happen in the movies. For example, in movies nobody has a problem finding a parking space even on the busiest of streets. Does anybody ever need the toilet in movieland and how do they manage it in those inconvenient costumes?

Close up: the classroom

- Make a list of things that happen in the real world but don't seem to happen in the movies.

- Make a second list of things that seem to be true in the movies but aren't in the real world.

- Does this tell us anything?

The use of film language and techniques in the Superhero movie rarely strays from the practices perfected by Hollywood back in the 1930s. Standard uses of the camera, continuity editing and so on are all directed towards making sure that once the audience has 'entered the world' of the film we are consumed by its narrative. It is especially vital to the Superhero movie that the audience is prepared to suspend their disbelief, otherwise audiences will just laugh when they ought to gasp.

How much will an audience accept?

Where audiences accept things that on reflection may be ridiculous or even contravene the laws of science, we talk about a 'suspension of disbelief'. It is only through enlisting Hollywood's familiar style of film-making that the film-maker has a chance of achieving this. But of course we all have different tolerance thresholds when it comes to believability.

If we look at Superhero movies, it is often the small details that add up to a convincing larger world. Often small visual 'explanations' are added to the films to answer oft-voiced criticisms of the character's realism. For example, in *The Incredible Hulk* (2008), we see Bruce Banner buying a pair of his iconic purple pants and examining them to make sure they are really stretchy, as people often wonder why all his clothes except his trousers tear off during his transformation; perhaps the tightness of his trousers goes someway to explaining the Hulk's less than even temper? All these small explanations help the audience to suspend their disbelief in order to 'go with' the movie.

All depictions of Superheroes raise questions around their credibility and hopefully have answers that fit with the 'reality' of the movie world in which it is set. The interesting question is: where is our threshold? How many 'doubts' occur to us as we are caught up in the action? Does the style of the film allow us to enjoy the fantasy without regard to the laws of physics?

Close up: the classroom

- Do any of these questions of 'credibility' matter when you watch a film? Why?

Perhaps uniquely to this genre there are often attempts to reflect the form of the comic book style on screen. Sometimes it is in small ways: in *Kick-Ass* it ranges from the small on-screen captions that are produced in a comic book style to the flashback history of Damon Macready (Big Daddy) and Mindy Macready (Hit Girl) shown in the form of an animated comic book, using the original art of John Romita Jr. as its basis.

Hulk (2003) went even further using both captions and split screen to give the film the visual look of a comic book. This technique, along with the film itself, was greeted with a mixed reception as many felt it was a gimmick rather than anything that improved the storytelling, even criticising it for drawing undue attention to the film's comic book roots.

Interestingly it highlights a common misconception that Superhero movies should be easy to make as all the director has to do is take the comic book away and shoot it as a ready-made storyboard. Although many comic book fans will be able to point to images on film that are versions of iconic panels lifted straight from the source, it is not as simple as this. They are both visual mediums but they do operate to different sets of rules.

The biggest differences lie in the fact that films are moving pictures with sound, whereas comic books are static and silent. Many of the conventions of comic books used to convey sound, motion and create impact are not suited to – or are unnecessary on – film. In comic books, sounds are conveyed by often extravagant, onomatopoeic exclamations that on film seem silly or merely comic. The original *Batman* TV series and film is a prime example of this. Movement is conveyed through exaggerated motion lines that are sometimes used on film but are largely unnecessary in a moving visual medium.

In comic books, the stature and power of the heroes and villains involves the use of very bright colours and extremely exaggerated musculatures, which tend to work against attempts to establish verisimilitude by the film-maker.

In general, comic books often contain sketchy detail and much narrative text that film does much better by 'showing' rather than 'telling'. Comics will also often contain large and complex panels that only work because the reader can pause and take time to absorb all that is happening. Pausing a film to replicate this depiction of complex and simultaneous events works against films' natural instinct to keep moving to maintain audience involvement. Editing is a more effective way of achieving the same effect on-screen.

Close up: the classroom

Look at the page from the *Daredevil* comic book below and the stills from the film, or better still the actual sequence from the film.

- How are they different?
- How are they similar?
- Is this important? Explain your answer.

7 & 8: Frames from *Daredevil* (2003) and the comic book that the sequence was based on (*Daredevil: The Man Without Fear*, 1982)

The films that most closely resemble their source materials are highly stylised and make for a much different viewing experience than 'normal' films. Over recent years the films based on the work of influential comic writer Frank Miller are the most striking examples of these. Although not strictly Superhero movies, *Sin City* (2005), *300* (2007) and *The Spirit* (2008) all take great pains to put the comic book on screen as far as is possible. As their style is very extreme, this means that this visual lack of compromise does work but the audience has no illusions that these stories are not taking place in the real world. In each case there are differing reasons for this. In *Sin City*, the comic book actively takes the filmic world of *film noir* and heightens its codes and conventions for dramatic effect. Any attempt on-screen to take this *noir* world 'back to reality' would entirely defeat the property's original purpose. In *300*, the imagery (as Frank Miller explained) is deliberately exaggerated 'to mythologise and emphasise' the legendary nature of the Spartans' sacrifice. It is in the less successful *The Spirit* where perhaps the process went a little too far. In Frank Miller's attempts to pay homage to the influence of the notable comic writer Will Eisner, the audience was confronted by an often confusing world that probably worked significantly better on paper than it did on film. Indeed, in *Kick-Ass* there is a brief visual joke at the expense of *The Spirit* as the cinema visited in the film is depicted showing *The Spirit 3*, not a very likely prospect in the 'real world'.

9: Reverential...   10: ... Mythologised...   11: ... a bit too far?

Close up: the exam

Style can be a very difficult idea to talk about. Keep things simple – 'realistic' and 'unrealistic' are useful terms here. Does the 'feel' of the film help or hinder your enjoyment? Are Superhero movies that different from other films?

What have we learnt?

In this chapter we have seen that:

- Although the Superhero movie is a relatively new genre, thanks to its source material it has not been slow in developing aspects of visual style that do mark it out from other genres.

- The style of the Superhero movie has adapted to cinema: the timeless struggle between the forces of light and the ever present shadow of the dark and its criminal denizens.

- In telling its story it never forgets the importance of convincing its audience, as the producers of the film that started it all understood all too well when they came up with the now immortal tagline: 'You'll believe a man can fly.'

Case Study 1

Spider-Man – A Superhero Movie Template?

Release date: 2002

Production: Marvel Entertainment

Producers: Laura Ziskin, Ian Bryce, Grant Curtis, Avi Arad, Stan Lee

Distribution: Columbia Pictures

Director: Sam Raimi

Screenplay: David Koepp, Scott Rosenberg (uncredited), Alvin Sargent (uncredited)

Comic by: Stan Lee and Steve Ditko

Publisher: Marvel

Main cast: Tobey Maguire, Willem Dafoe, Kirsten Dunst, James Franco, Cliff Robertson, Rosemary Harris, J. K. Simmons

Music: Danny Elfman

Budget: $140 million

Box-office: $821,708,551

Tagline: *With great power comes great responsibility* or *Go for the ultimate spin!*

Synopsis

Peter Parker is the archetype of the bullied science nerd who can only dream about getting the girl. His life is changed forever when he is bitten by a genetically enhanced spider. His new powers seem a straightforward boon at first but his attempt to win money to buy a car to impress Mary Jane soon proves how complicated life can be as a Superhero. In allowing a robber to escape, his uncle Ben is killed. He blames himself and decides to atone for this by using his powers for good assuming the identity of Spider-Man. Enter the Green Goblin, who has a different idea about the exercise of power. The burden of great power and great responsibility then rapidly begins to reveal itself to the conflicted Peter Parker.

Spider-Man as an Example Of the Genre

Introduction

Spider-Man in many ways is one of the classic Superhero stories. By far the most popular hero to emerge from the Silver Age 1960s, it is the first popular story to put a teenager at the centre of the narrative. As with the film industry of the present day, Stan Lee understood who his audience was – not children but teenagers with all the problems and angst that come with that time of life. In embodying these troubles in a Superhero, Spider-Man was able to reach out to an audience in a way the godlike Superman and super-rich Batman could not. In terms of codes and conventions, Spider-Man both follows and sets the standard.

Setting

As is traditional with most Superhero Movies, the time period is contemporary. Spider-Man may have begun his career in the mid-to-late 1960s, but he continues to web-sling in today's world and the film reflects this to keep it realistic and relatable for today's audiences.

The setting is urban where there is no shortage of criminals for our hero to find. More than this, it is the classic Marvel setting of New York (or a variation on it) where many of their heroes (Daredevil, Fantastic Four) have a home or base. In terms of specific locations there is the High School where Peter Parker first struggles with his powers; and there is the laboratory and boardroom so often the 'breeding ground' for villainy. Above all, though, for Spider-Man we have the iconic image of Spidey joyfully web-slinging between the canyon-like skyscrapers of New York, reproduced convincingly for the first time on screen.

Themes

The themes of responsibility, secret identity, emotional conflict and how hard it can be to do the right thing and more are present. Responsibility goes to the very heart of Peter Parker / Spider-Man's character as he feels personally responsible for his uncle Ben's death. Ben's near final words to Peter of 'with great power comes great responsibility' echo through both Peter's guilt and popular culture in general. Emotional conflict and the need to protect his loved ones from further danger are all bound up in his secret identity and Peter struggles with the demands of being a High School student by day and the heroic crime fighter by night.

Characters

In Spider-Man we have the full range of Superhero movie characters. The hero, Peter Parker / Spider-Man, is typically flawed and shares many of our problems with everyday life that even super powers cannot solve. The villain, Norman Osborne / Green Goblin, strives for himself at great cost to others but is not entirely without redeeming features and is mentally afflicted by the process that created his powers. His son, Harry Osborne, is Peter Parker's friend and a side-swapper in the making. This process starts in earnest at the film's conclusion when he swears revenge on Spider-Man, his father's apparent killer, but only becomes complete in *Spider-Man 3*, when he returns to the side of good and sacrifices himself to save Spider-Man and Mary Jane. We have a strong woman in the form of an apparently frail Aunt May who becomes Peter Parker's anchor in his rapidly changing life. Mary Jane acts as an unwitting supporter in her belief in Peter and admiration for Spider-Man. J Jonah Jameson is a typical authority figure who distrusts this new Superhero and sets out to 'expose' him, despite how many newspapers he helps to sell. Finally, the public is there aplenty, cheerleading for the new hero's attempt to defend them from New York's criminal element; they consider Spidey 'one of us'. We see this as they throw assorted debris at the Green Goblin in an attempt to help Spider-Man, two members of the public shouting: 'You mess with Spidey, you mess with New York!' and 'You mess with one of us, you mess with all of us!' This is a measure of the esteem in which they hold Spider-Man and a veiled reference to the events of 9/11 2001.

Iconography

Much of the iconography we associate with Superhero movies is on display, including the iconic costume and Peter Parker's trademark camera. We also have gadgets aplenty for the Green Goblin, his glider and pumpkin bombs being amongst the more notable props. More than these details is the use of New York and the Stars and Stripes, ensuring there is no mistake about who and what Spider-Man protects and represents.

Narrative

The narrative is an origin story, a pattern followed by virtually all other Superhero movies, with seeds being sown for possible sequels. We see Peter bitten by the genetically enhanced spider and go through the process of coming to terms with his newly acquired powers. We see a change in Harry Osborne that may or may not lead to him following in his father's villainous footsteps. We are also introduced to Dr. Curt Connors, one of Peter's lecturers, who may or may not become The Lizard in a sequel.

Style

The style owes much to the original comic book. It is dynamic and fast-paced during the action, which is successfully augmented by good use of CGI so we again 'believe a man can fly'– or at least web-sling. Alongside the readily recognisable visual elements we have a typical Superhero musical score by Danny Elfman (no stranger to Superhero movies having *Batman* (1989), *Batman Returns* (1992) and *Darkman* (1990) under his belt already at this point). It is a sweepingly heroic orchestral score; in its use of distinct themes for each of the main protagonists it follows very much in the pattern laid out by John Williams in the original *Superman* score.

Summary

If we are looking for a Superhero movie that comes close to defining the genre then we could do worse than consult our 'friendly neighborhood Spider-Man'.

Chapter 5 Narrative and Plot

In this chapter we will cover:

- Narrative and plot.
- How are Superhero movies typically structured?
- Do they have any formulas?

12: *Wolverine*, whose narrative is the subject of X-Men spin-off *X-Men Origins: Wolverine* (2009)

The Superhero Movie – Telling The Story

The narrative and plot of Superhero movies is often referred to as a formula or **formulaic**. Many Superhero movies are felt to be the same film with a new 'cape' and a different cast. In such a typical mainstream genre, this observation is to some extent true. Our job in analysing narrative and plot in the Superhero movie is to find and understand the components of this criticism and decide when it is fair and when it is unfair.

As we have seen in Chapter 1, in the most basic terms a **narrative** is the story and the **plot** is how this story is constructed. 'Basic' is a good term to use here as one of the criticisms levelled at Superhero movies (and other blockbuster genres) is that the story is predictable and the plots are repetitive. This may be true but we need to consider the narrative and plot that is present.

Most Superhero movies have a linear narrative that leads up to a final confrontation with the villain. In *Spider-Man*, we begin with voice-over from Peter Parker, who is about to tell his story, that, despite the

Key terms

Formulaic: Where a film contains the same ingredients as others.

Narrative: The story of a film and how it is constructed.

Plot: The more detailed plan of how the story is constructed in the film.

confrontation with the Green Goblin, it's 'all about a girl'. We then get a fairly linear narrative that establishes how Peter Parker became Spider-Man and the effect this has had upon his life and relationships. Within this story are several sub-plots, like his relationship with Mary Jane, Aunt May and Harry Osborn, some of which continue through to the third film. A prime example of this is that Peter does not reveal his role in the death of his Uncle Ben to Aunt May until the second film. She then shows Peter through her example how to deal positively with such situations. This role is then changed fundamentally with developments in the third film in which Peter finally learns both the ultimate lesson of – and how to deal with – his uncle's death. With such aspects of plotting across all three movies, it is a good example of how the narrative of a Superhero movie is not as one-dimensional as the critics say.

This said, *Spider-Man* is an example of one kind of formulaic narrative common to most, if not all, Superhero movie franchises – the 'origin' story.

The 'formula'

The nearest to an identifiable formula within the Superhero movie is the need to tell the hero's 'origin' story. The first film in any Superhero franchise usually lays out for the general audience how the hero acquired their powers. The Hollywood producers seem to adopt this as a default position for the first film, either as an easy way to structure it or perhaps through a lack of confidence in the source material's wider acceptance. After all, who does not know that Superman came from Krypton or that Spider-Man was bitten by a radioactive (now a genetically altered) spider? Perhaps more importantly, this is now what an audience expects from the genre.

There are some notable exceptions, such as in *X-Men*, where Wolverine's origins are not explored. *X-Men 2* (2003) is dominated by his own search for his origin and it is only in a third film (the fourth of the franchise) where the full story of Wolverine's origins is told (in the instructively titled *X-Men Origins: Wolverine* [2009]).

Of the other two narrative forms we have previously mentioned, circular and episodic narratives are less common. *Sin City* is perhaps the only clear example in the Superhero genre of an episodic narrative where separate stories involving separate characters eventually converge during the film. This partly reflects the way separate stories from Frank Miller's original comic have been combined within the movie's narrative.

There are some examples of circular narrative (at least partially). *Daredevil* starts with the film's story almost complete and goes back to show us how and why he got to the situation he now faces. Another example is *Kick-Ass*, in which the central character narrates his story in hindsight. Although visually we begin with an image part way through the story, it is being narrated from its end and is at least partially circular.

A point of criticism often raised when dealing with Superheroes is that the audience knows that they won't die and this renders any jeopardy they are placed in unconvincing. The important distinction to make here is that we may know this is a decades-old character that has never died (they are sometimes beaten) but *the characters do not know this*. We can still therefore share vicariously in their jeopardy, which is perhaps the most we can do when 'enjoying' the depiction of any extreme situation on-screen.

Other Narrative Features

In terms of narrative viewpoint, the Superhero movie typically has the audience share the point of view of the hero. This is a mix of both **omniscient and restrictive viewpoints** as we know more than most of the 'average' characters in the film but there are often things we don't know because the hero does not know them either. Typically we will have an omniscient point of view as we know who the villain is and how they are plotting against the hero. Our enjoyment is not through figuring out a mystery but through anticipating how our heroes will meet the challenge we can see looming before them, even if they cannot.

Other narrative techniques can also be found from time to time such as **flashback** and **parallel narratives**. In *The Fantastic Four*, we get occasional flashbacks to the time before they became Superheroes. For a while, Dr Doom's story runs parallel to theirs as he is drawn to villainy and the heroes are drawn towards good.

The other aspects of narrative we have discussed in Part 1 are not used with any frequency in Superhero movies. Ellipsis and the use of time and space are used in a fairly standard way in constructing the narrative.

Key terms

Omniscient Narrative: A narrative which allows us to know more about the characters and their situations than they know themselves.

Restricted Narratives: A narrative that only allows us to know what the characters know.

Flashback: Where a character remembers past events in order to show the audience what happened.

Parallel Narratives: When two or more characters share different stories that centre on the same event.

Close up: the classroom

Invent an origin story for your own Superhero.

- Does it matter if the Superhero's origin is explained in a movie of your idea?
- Why might we keep a Superhero's origin secret from the audience?
- How might the audience respond to this?

Superhero movies: new genre, old stories?

13: *Ghost Rider* (2007): Peter Fonda as Mephistopheles, legendary on so many levels

A comparison that is often made when discussing Superheroes is with more ancient myths and legends. There are direct examples in film, such as *Thor* (2011). In the comic books many other characters from ancient myths, legends and classic stories are common visitors. For example, Hercules makes an appearance in the Marvel universe along with Dracula; and Ares, the god of war, appears in both the Marvel and DC universes. It is also observed that the morals and themes of many Superhero stories act as fables.

An example that embraces both classic and modern is *Ghost Rider*, which is largely a re-working of the Faustian bargain-with-the-devil story. Johnny Blaze, played by Nicholas Cage, agrees to work for Mephistopheles, played by Peter Fonda, in order to cure his father of cancer. His father is then killed in a stunt soon after, a typical trick played by the Devil on Johnny. The narrative then involves Johnny's motives for making his deal with the Devil as well as his attempts to get out of it. Unusually he succeeds and Mephistopheles offers to take back the Ghost Rider curse. In a twist on the responsibility theme, Johnny turns him down in order to 'own' the curse and turn its power against Mephistopheles wherever he can.

The Superhero narrative theme of responsibility is present from the start. Johnny's father chides him, 'When you do things without thinking, you ain't making a choice. The choice is making you' adding, 'Choices have consequences'. He says this as he lights up another cigarette, the irony of which is not lost on the audience.

Perhaps most interestingly for this topic is the voice-over that ends the film:

> **They say that the west was built on legends, and that legends are a way of understanding things greater than ourselves. Forces that shape our lives. Events that defy explanation. Individuals whose lives soar to the heavens or fall to earth. This is how legends are born.**

Not just an explanation of legends but of Superheroes as well, perhaps?

Close up: the classroom

Research what other characters from older stories, myths and legends have appeared in Superhero stories.

- Which have not been used? Why do you think this is?
- If you were to base a Superhero on an already existing character, who would it be and why?

Close up: creative work

Write a short pitch for a film featuring the character you created in the previous activity.

What have we learnt?

In this chapter:

- We should have realised that like all genres there is inevitably repetition; even storylines are used and re-used over and over.
- We need to look a little deeper and see how even the origin story can be made fresh and interesting if handled by good writers and a creative director.
- We have realised that perhaps it is not that important how similar many of these narratives are. What is more important is how the re-telling of these stories is adapted to address our times and our stories.

Chapter 6 Themes

In this chapter we will cover:

- What do we mean by a theme?
- What themes do we typically find in Superhero movies?
- How are these themes handled?
- How important are they to the genre?

Close up: the exam

When you look at the themes present in a film try to keep track of which themes are popular in different films.

The Superhero movie – What else does it say?

14: *The Punisher* (2004): Frank Castle assesses the damage to his kitchen

The **themes** of any film are the issues and subjects that they deal with aside from the main story. Sometimes these are the actual things the film-maker wishes to discuss and the story of the hero is a means to that end. This often prompts the observation that Superheroes are like the myths and legends of ancient times whose stories often contained a lesson to teach or a moral to impart. For a mainstream Hollywood genre the Superhero movie is relatively rich in themes, and most of those

Key terms

Themes: Ideas and stories that are associated with a particular genre.

discussed in this section can be found in most of the Superhero movies we see. These themes tend to split into those centered on the 'private' or the individual and those centered on the 'public' or 'bigger picture' brought into focus by the film. As previously we will look at the most common, as a complete list could be *very* long and defeat the point of trying to find things that films in a genre have in common.

Close up: the classroom

What themes do you think should be/are present in the modern Superhero movie?

- Compile a class list; try to rank them in importance.
- Record your ideas to look at again later.

The Superhero movie and the Individual: the 'private'

Motivations

Many of the themes based on individual motivation can be summarised by the central question of 'Why do they do what they do?' Both the hero and the audience will question the motivation behind the decision to fight crime in the way that they do. Surely with the power superheroes have there is an even greater need for formal training and the backing of an organisation such as the police force or government? The answer to this question leads us into ideology, which we will look at in the next section.

Revenge

One of the most common motivations for the hero's fight against crime is that of revenge, at least initially. The desire to avenge the death of loved ones is often the first step on the road to a wider mission. A long list including *Batman*, *The Punisher*, *Daredevil* and *Blade* all began through the death of at least one family member. However, most move on from this thirst for 'personal justice' to embrace a wider, more universal desire to do good in exercising the powers they have been gifted.

Truth, Justice (and the American Way)

The now famous Spider-Man maxim of 'With great power comes great responsibility' is pertinent to virtually all Superhero stories.

These characters are heroes because of how they shoulder this responsibility in their mission to help people (particularly the defenceless). This stands as an idealistic contrast to many real-life powerful figures who often pop up as caricatures and who are frequently seen to use this power to help themselves. Again, many of the top examples such as the X-Men, Spider-Man, The Fantastic Four act from this idealistic form of motivation.

There are two very famous 'special' cases absent from this list who are less motivated and more compelled as embodiments of more explicitly American values – Superman and Captain America, who will be considered in more detail in the ideology section. Kick-Ass, who has no real super-powers, jokes at one point that 'with no power comes no responsibility'. But even he 'falls in line', realising that this is not true and in reality we all have responsibilities, including Superheroes.

Self-preservation and Self-sacrifice

In the case of the Hulk, we see a noble mix of two other individual motivations. Bruce Banner goes on the run to protect himself from the attentions of the US military; his choice of isolated locations also contains an element of self-sacrifice as this makes his quest for a cure for his condition much more difficult. Most heroes' decisions involve some element of self-sacrifice as they have to give up any chance of normality if they are to use their powers for good. In a less altruistic vein, the X-Men being an example of this, heroes act to protect humanity so that they are seen as a force for good rather than freakish outcasts to be persecuted because of their abilities.

Redemption

Redemption, making good for previous wrongs, is a theme most associated with evil in the Superhero movie and it crosses the divide between hero and villain. We have traditional acts of redemption such as Harry Osborn's sacrifice to save Spider-Man at the end of *Spider-Man 3*, although Peter Parker has various things to atone for in this film as well. We also see the hero Iron Man as Tony Stark's attempt to atone for the harm he has caused as an arms manufacturer, although it is almost his undoing as Obadiah Stane is far from accepting of Stark Industries' new direction. Given Stark's personality there are plenty of things for him to atone for in *Iron Man 2* as well, not least his arrogance as he declares he has 'privatised world peace'.

Relationships

These are a vital component in the Superhero movie in extending it beyond the confines of the 'big bang' special effect. As in any film, all kinds of relationships feature – friendship, enmity, love...

Most typical is the love theme, both romantic and in relation to family. Love can be straightforward and textbook, such as Hellboy's love for Liz Sherman in *Hellboy* and *Hellboy II* (2008). Here we have a couple that have a typical Superhero relationship that is complicated by both their powers and their circumstances. This tends to be the case with virtually all romantic relationships in Superhero movies; nothing is ever as simple as the traditional 'boy meets girl...'. If we list some of the couples, the 'course of true love' never runs smooth and varies only in its complexity. Superman and Lois Lane; Peter Parker and Mary Jane; Dave and Katie – all have secret identity 'issues' where the hero can't voice his feelings as he is afraid it could place his other half in danger.

We have the pressures of the situation as well as fame that continually hamper Reed and Sue's wedding plans in *Fantastic Four*. In *X-Men* there is an almost traditional love triangle between Jean Grey, Wolverine and Cyclops, where she is torn between the wild and the stable.

Most common perhaps is how the obsession or mission gets in the way of the couple, as with Daredevil and Elektra and most obviously in *Batman*, where Bruce Wayne steadfastly remains alone. Perhaps the most 'difficult' relationship of all can be found in *Hancock* where the characters have to make a straight choice between being together and their mission to protect humanity. If Hancock and Mary Embrey are together for any length of time, their powers will disappear, placing them and the world in jeopardy.

Family, both real and constructed, is also important. Real family members provide support and motivation. Where would Spider-Man be without the influence of his aunt and uncle? Would Johnny Storm even know Reed Richards if he wasn't Sue Storm's brother? Thor provides the antithesis of this with father-son-brother issues of inter-galactic proportions. More often, though, the 'family' in a Superhero movie is the team that they are in (*X-Men* and *Fantastic Four*) or the people the heroes surround themselves with (*Batman* or *Iron Man*). Whatever kind of family we are dealing with, it allows us on this personal level to recognise issues that we can identify with, as most members of the audience are part of a family of one kind or another. The relationship issues in the Superhero movie are almost as important as the story itself and they are the themes that give the audience its most common form of emotional 'hook' into the story.

The moral question

One theme that all Superheroes have to deal with is the moral question of the right and wrong of their actions and whether their 'transgression' in the cause of good is right or wrong. We almost have a 'scale of conscience' here. At one end we have the angst-ridden self-doubt of Spider-Man and at the other end of the scale the extreme unswerving belief of The Punisher. In between, there lies the public debate of Hancock's approach to crime fighting. Ultimately the audience will have to judge the hero's actions for themselves, just one example of how a theme can engage interest.

Choices

Following on from morality's ability to engage the audience is perhaps the most fundamental 'private' theme of all – that of the choices the heroes have to make. The heroes (and villains) may be confronted with extreme choices but the principle of making these decisions applies to us all. 'What would I do?' is often a question that the film-maker is hoping the audience will ask itself. The decisions are never easy and we are starkly reminded of the consequences they can have. When Superman gives up his powers in *Superman II* to become the ordinary Clark Kent it begins with a beating in a bar and ends with General Zod's conquest of the world. Now, when we choose our subjects in Year 9, we don't expect those kinds of consequence but it will affect our immediate future nevertheless.

Making choices is something all members of the audience can sympathise with and is an integral part of the Superhero movie's appeal.

Close up: the classroom

Choose a Superhero movie.

- Make a list of the decisions the Superhero has to make or the situations they face in the private aspect of their lives.
- Choose one of these and 'put yourself in their shoes'. What options do they have?
- Which one would you choose, explain why and try to discuss the consequences it may have.

The Superhero movie and society: the 'public'

As with many films, Superhero movies address wider issues and topics of public interest and debate. This has been true throughout the history of cinema as films are ultimately products of the times in which they are made. We will consider some of those that recur most often within this genre.

Right and wrong

A major 'public' theme that follows on directly from a 'private' one concerns the discussion of right and wrong. The effectiveness and fairness of the legal system is often called into question, accusations of corruption in *Batman Begins* (2005) and *Kick-Ass* being two examples of this.

Superheroes often pursue what could be best described as 'natural justice': in other words they 'take the law into their own hands' tackling and punishing wrongdoers outside the bounds of the legal system. This is what is known as being a vigilante and in everyday society this is not seen as a good thing. Superhero movies justify this by often making the criminal challenge much greater than what normal authorities can cope with, hence the presence of the super villain; we have seen what happens when the police try to arrest Magneto. They will also depict the hero's actions as receiving public acclaim and approval – 'Go, Spidey, go!' The Superhero (most of the time) will stop short of killing and hands over their defeated enemy to the normal police (think of all those criminals hanging from lamp posts by spider webs). The debate remains as to the questionable role of the vigilante: The Daily Bugle regularly turns public opinion against Spider-Man and it is the actions of Batman that are ultimately blamed for the Joker's reign of terror over Gotham City in *The Dark Knight*. The 'need' for these individuals who act outside of normal controls is a continued debate and encompasses aspects of ideology that we will consider in the next chapter.

Discrimination

As superheroes are a very small, admittedly powerful minority, the differing aspects of discrimination are a common theme. The *X-Men* films are key texts in this discussion. We are introduced to Magneto outside the Auschwitz concentration camp, the culmination of the racist policies of the Nazis and their 'final solution'. The discrimination against the X-Men mutants is often compared to society's attitudes towards sexuality over recent decades, their 'condition' being dealt with as a disease to be cured, much like homosexuality still is in some quarters. We also see a positive representation of the disabled as the leader of the X-Men, the wise and telepathic Professor Xavier, conducts operations from his wheelchair.

Representations are not all positive and some still reflect general issues within Hollywood film-making. Whilst there are female Superheroes equal in power to their male counterparts, they are much less common, objectified by their costumes (although the men are too) and have yet to provide us with a successful female Superhero franchise in its own right. Is Wonder Woman waiting in the wings to save this day?

Close up: the classroom

Look at the poster for *Iron Man 2* (2010).

- What representations do we see there?

- Which are positive and which are negative? Are any neither?

- If you have seen the film, are your perceptions of these representations different from people that have only seen the poster?

15: *Iron Man 2* poster

Social Class

What we refer to as 'class' in the UK is the more simple distinction of rich and poor in the largely American Superhero movie. The heroes themselves come from diverse backgrounds, from the super-rich Bruce Wayne through multiple middle-class X-Men to the much poorer Peter Parker. Despite the fact they are mostly engaged in a struggle to defend the poor against criminals and predatory corporations, many of the protagonists come from an equally poor background. This grey area of debate is illustrated by the redeeming feature given to the Sandman in *Spider-Man 3*, when it is revealed that his criminal motivation is to pay his daughter's hospital bills. This does not justify his crimes but makes him sympathetic enough for Peter Parker to forgive him and for the audience to accept this. Perhaps the solution to this villainy is not the expensive and destructive confrontations on the streets of New York but state-funded health care?

Science and Technology

Our relationship with these two, particularly our suspicion and distrust of them, has been ever-present in Superhero movies. In the original 1960s comic books it was the fear of nuclear radiation that spawned many heroes and villains; these days it is the cutting edge science of genetics that is the source for many narratives. Spider-Man is again a good example of this: in the original comic he is bitten by a radioactive spider but in the more recent film version it is a genetically engineered super-spider that does the damage.

Technology is seen both as a threat when misused and a saviour when used for good. Nowhere is this contrasting use of technology more closely examined than in the *Iron Man* films. Tony Stark initially revels in his nickname 'the merchant of death'; his sales pitch for his weaponry is unrepentant:

> **They say that the best weapon is the one you never have to fire. I respectfully disagree. I prefer the weapon you only have to fire once. That's how Dad did it, that's how America does it, and it's worked out pretty well so far. I present to you the newest in Stark Industries' Freedom line. Find an excuse to let one of these off the chain, and I personally guarantee, the bad guys won't even wanna come out of their caves. Ladies and gentlemen, for your consideration... the Jericho.**

But when some of his products are used on him and the soldiers escorting him, Stark realises that somebody is selling to both sides to increase conflict and, in turn, profit. We may wonder how this should be much of a revelation for the super genius he is supposed to be.

Perhaps in giving him the benefit of the doubt we too are guilty of the old maxim about 'seeing what we want to see'. He acts upon this epiphany by immediately suspending all Stark weapons production on his return from captivity and it is perhaps at this point we see most clearly that this is fiction – or perhaps not, as the shareholders (in the form of Obadiah Stane) react with deadly force.

Nevertheless, for every doomsday weapon and death ray there are shields and gadgets to help combat them, so what is important is really who uses the technology and how.

Society

The Superhero movie touches on many other areas of society that are sometimes the subject of our fears and suspicions. Our occasional disquiet at war and the military often leads them to be portrayed as both deliberate and unwitting protagonists. Economics and politics can feature too; Aunt May has her house repossessed in *Spider-Man 2* and Tony Stark faces a hostile government at a congressional hearing in *Iron Man 2*. There are other examples of how 'the establishment' is viewed with distrust and some critics suggest this is a reflection of Hollywood's supposed long-held liberal (left-wing) stance. Equally, there are as many critics who hold the opposite views and see the Superhero as a *right-wing* figure who acts above the law often in the interests of 'the establishment'. Batman and Superman have found themselves on either side of this argument, particularly in their comic book incarnations.

Close up: the classroom

Choose a Superhero movie.

- Make a list of the 'public' themes it deals with.
- Decide as a group which one of these is most important.

Either:

- Organise a debate based on this issue.

Or

- Explain what the film has to say about this issue. Remember to say what you think of both the film's point of view and your own opinion about it.

What have we learnt?

In this chapter we have seen that:

- There are a number of common themes that act to unify the genre.

- In looking for themes in the Superhero movie we find many different ones with differing levels of meaning for different audiences. They continue to operate on the contrasting levels of 'the private' and 'the public'.

- Perhaps the incredible extent of the hero's abilities compared to the 'limitations' of a normal individual make the contrast sharper.

- One thing is almost for sure (as sure as you can be with these things): at least one of these themes will have an impact on even the most unconcerned spectator. Even the thrill seeker who may only have gone to 'watch the fireworks' that the 'big bang' of Superhero special effects offers cannot escape their effect.

Chapter 7 Ideology

In this chapter we will cover:

- What is ideology?

- What ideologies can we find in Superhero movies?

- How different ideology can lead to different films.

- How a changing world has changed the ideology of the Superhero movie.

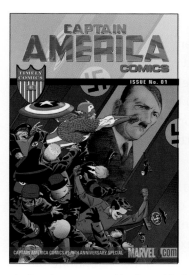

16: Comics covers – Ideology: Nuff Said?

As most of the Superhero movies are American, their national **ideology** is ever-present. Spider-Man is framed against the stars and stripes at least once in all three movies (to date). In most Superhero movies, American leadership and supremacy comes to the fore. It is usually up to them, and their heroes, to 'save the world'. A number of films exemplify this – *Superman*, *X-Men* (with a few international additions), *Blade* and the *Fantastic Four* all act to save the world as Americans on our behalf. In all of these, the 'can do' heroism and a return to almost pioneer style values of the old frontier come to the fore.

This kind of 'flying the flag' for the USA often draws a lot of criticism (including in America) for being over the top. Nevertheless it remains an easily spotted form of ideology that is a very important driving force for many of these movies.

> **Key terms**
>
> **Ideology:** A system of values, beliefs or ideas that is common to specific group of people.

Superman and Captain America are two characters who genuinely believe in truth, justice and 'the American way' alongside life, liberty and the pursuit of happiness. Superman embodies this ethos as a mixture of sacred Kryptonian mission and an idyllic mid-West upbringing – a Superman for a superpower, perhaps? Captain America, a volunteer and sole product of a World War 2 super soldier program, is a walking, talking embodiment of the 'Why we fight' values of America's 'Greatest Generation'. It is interesting that during the 1970s – the era of Watergate and US withdrawal from Vietnam – he hung up his shield and became Nomad, and in more recent political turbulence he found himself fighting his own government and being assassinated – symbolically absenting his values from the modern era, perhaps? (This is an example of equivalence between a Marvel and a DC character, one being in some ways a version of the other. Can you spot any others?)

The pioneer values of the 'old West' are nowhere better exemplified in what has been described as the American 'cult of the individual'. One hero sheriff or gunfighter takes it upon themselves to 'make a difference'. In pursuing their vigilante mission to 'clean up the streets', the Superhero follows in a long tradition that continues on from Western characters through 'rogue' individuals in contemporary urban dramas, such as 'Dirty' Harry Callahan.

Many other ideologies are touched upon and impact the Superhero movie in less obvious ways. Freedom, another cherished American value, is used as a justification and talking point in some of these films, the actions of Superheroes being seen as an exercising of their right to act in a free country. In *Iron Man* we see Stark's perspective change on this issue as he starts the film defending American freedom through the traditional means of force of arms. Once he has had his 'epiphany' he withdraws his armaments and acts alone, using his newly invented armoured suit, despite his government's attempts to acquire it for themselves.

Terrorism and government attempts to combat it through limiting its citizen's freedoms are themes that feature in *V For Vendetta* (2006), *The Dark Knight* and others. Religious ideologies are also not without their uses – the producers of *Superman* openly acknowledged the biblical parallels of Jor-El sending his only son to earth to save us all.

Close up: the exam

Ideology can be a controversial area open to much debate. Consider if it is a good or a bad thing for movies to deal with. What about your ideas? Do you agree or disagree? Have you changed or picked up any ideas from films?

Close up: the classroom

- How different are the ideas in the different films you have seen?

- Why are they different? Is there anything else they should talk about?

- How important do you think ideology is to the enjoyment or success of Superhero movies? Does it matter to you?

What have we learnt?

In this chapter we have seen that:

- In some ways ideology is 'where you find it' as different audiences will recognise different values dependent on their own perspectives.

- Overall the Superhero movie strongly features a general ideology that there is a 'right way' and a 'wrong way' to behave.

- Whether inspired by law, religion, ideas or indeed the films themselves, it may be up to our heroes and indeed us to find it for ourselves.

Case Study 2

V For Vendetta – Themes And Ideology As Narrative?

Release date: 2006

Production: Warner Bros., Virtual Studios, Silver Pictures

Producers: Joel Silver, Larry Wachowski,

Andy Wachowski, Grant Hill

Distribution: Warner Bros.

Director: James McTeigue

Screenplay: Larry Wachowski, Andy Wachowski

Comic by: Alan Moore (uncredited), David Lloyd

Publisher: UK Quality Comics, USA

Vertigo (DC Comics)

Main cast: Natalie Portman, Hugo Weaving, Stephen Rea, John Hurt, Steven Fry

Music: Dario Marianelli

Budget: $54 million

Box-office: $132,511,035

Tagline: *Freedom! Forever!*

Synopsis

V, a mysterious figure disguised as Guy Fawkes, rescues Evey Hammond from a group of 'Fingermen', government-sanctioned toughs. From then on their fates become entwined as V pursues his campaign of unrest and revenge waged against an oppressive fascist state. Evey in many ways has a longer journey to make as she struggles to find herself in this 'harsh new world'. V's murderous plots come to head with revolution in the air, the fall of a dictator and the symbolic destruction of the Houses of Parliament.

Introduction

Although there are certainly precedents for heroes that find themselves in conflict with their government (for example, Captain America in the recent *Civil War* comic storyline from 2006-07), *V For Vendetta*'s narrative gives us perhaps the Superhero movie's richest example of challenging themes and ideologies.

Themes – The Private

Motivations

V's motivations are a complex mix of both the public and the private. When we first meet him it seems that a basic sense of natural justice and a desire to protect the innocent drive his actions as he steps in to save Evey Hammond from the corrupt and violent Fingermen. Yet soon after, his larger motivation begins to be revealed: to take on the totalitarian state that has oppressed Britain and to prompt a revolution against it through a series of carefully planned symbolic terrorist acts. As more of his character is revealed we discover the motivation that is possibly most central to the understanding of V.

Revenge

Alongside his program of terrorism is his quest for revenge on those whose experiments abused him and his fellow detainees at the Larkhill detention centre where he was held. One by one he has murdered all the people who worked there in authority. Even the sympathetic Dr. Delia Surridge, who had gone someway to redeeming herself by showing remorse for her involvement, accepts her fate as a final act of atonement for her complicity in the crimes of the state. These acts of vengeance in some ways can be seen as righting a small wrong in comparison to the larger wrong of the Norsefire dictatorship, the fall of which, along with Chancellor Sutler's death, will be V's ultimate and much larger act of revenge.

Self-preservation and Self-sacrifice

There are elements of both of these themes in V's Superhero activities. His kidnapping and imprisonment of Evey is an act of self-preservation to begin with, especially after she has escaped his clutches and considered giving herself up. After he has 'conditioned' her to be free he is prepared to take the risk of letting her go, which could result in the destruction of both himself and his cause. Ultimately he knows that he will not survive all that he has planned but is willing to make this sacrifice in order to see it through to a successful revolution.

Responsibility

Responsibility is also a theme dealt with in *V For Vendetta* and covers the whole range, from the responsibility of individuals for their own actions – and inactions – all the way up to holding an oppressive government accountable for murder and oppression. Nowhere more clearly is this demonstrated than through the character of Evey Hammond, who gradually takes responsibility for her own life and ultimately shares responsibility for the revolution when she sends V on his way by starting the train that will ignite beneath the Houses of Parliament.

Redemption

In such a morally murky narrative as we have here, redemption is not always easy to find. In some ways, V is 'redeemed' when Detective Chief Inspector Eric Finch, the officer tracking him down, realises V's actions are intended for a greater good; indeed as a prominent officer of the oppressive state he is somewhat redeemed himself by not stopping Evey from launching the final bomb towards Parliament. Perhaps the clearest redemption is that of the population who wake from their slumber, abandoning their pubs and TV sets to stand against their government and symbolically state 'enough is enough' at the film's climax. The faces of the regime's victims, prominent in the crowd, signify that their deaths have not been in vain and that they have finally received some measure of justice.

Relationships

Even in a film that so prominently deals with many larger themes, individual relationships are still important. We see how cruel the state has become in the telling of Valerie Page's story of her lesbian relationship leading to her detention and death. Perhaps most crucial is the relationship between V and Evey, and how both develop through being with one another. It can never be a traditional romance but from it V gains a deeper understanding of what it is he is fighting for and Evey learns the true value of freedom and the kind of adult responsibilities that come with it.

The moral question

For V, a Superhero who is a product of a government's experiments on its own people, things have gone beyond the 'friendly neighborhood' style of vigilante action. Many of his actions are justified by the old adage 'the ends justify the means'; overall we understand why he takes the moral stance he does without necessarily agreeing with all of his actions, which frequently result in mayhem and calculated murder. This makes him quite different from more traditional Superheroes whose morality is much more clearly in line with our own.

Choices

Although V's choices are clear and in some ways limited by his personal circumstances, the theme of choice does feature strongly for many characters in the film. Evey's spur of the moment choice to obstruct his capture leads her into a world where there are many more choices to make. Overall, however, in addressing the public at large we are reminded that choosing to do nothing – apathy – is still a choice, and one that has consequences just as powerful as any other course of (in)action.

Themes – The Public

Right and wrong

A major 'public' theme that follows on directly from a 'private' one concerns the discussion of right and wrong. V does many things that we would usually consider to be wrong, murder being an obvious example. It is easy for us to feel that the bullying Prothero and the vile Bishop Lilliman deserve their fates but it's not as easy to see this in the case of the remorseful Dr. Delia Surridge. Nevertheless, all are illegally killed. Through this and others of V's actions we are invited to consider an eternal question – are these 'smaller' crimes justified in waging a 'just war' against a bigger evil?

Discrimination

Here we see the ultimate consequences of discrimination taken to its logical extremes. Several minority groups are 'removed' from normal society, political opponents, homosexuals and religious minorities being some of the named examples. In Valerie Page's story we see how this discrimination starts with the dismissal of her sexuality as a phase by her teacher through parental rejection, unemployment, bricks through windows to her ultimate detention and death.

Social Class

The importance of class is perhaps a more subtle issue than many of the other themes, but as this is a film set in England it does provide an ever-present backdrop. We see the working class, happy with their security, pubs and TVs, the middle classes more attuned to the tyranny but with too much to lose to act, and the ruling classes who use their position to consolidate both their wealth and power. We should consider how far these are stereotypes and how far they are an accurate reflection of the audience's attitudes.

Science and Technology

This Superhero movie theme is fairly traditional in its execution – science and technology are abused and put to evil use by the villains. Yet in their search for a virus and its antidote, an accident creates a superhero that will ultimately right this wrong. V is in this respect in the tradition of a Frankenstein-like monster that comes back to haunt its creators.

Society and Politics

The themes dealt with in *V For Vendetta* are very clearly issues that are of public concern and continuing discussion. V is not the conventional Superhero who very seldom kills and who acts within the broad control of the law. *V for Vendetta* is a contemporary reworking of a graphic novel inspired by the politics of the 1980s and the effects of Thatcherism. It deals with many issues which are very current, prime amongst which is just how authoritarian we will allow our government to become in order to keep its citizens 'safe'. With stricter anti-terrorism laws and increasing police powers it is an important question for us to ask ourselves.

In the film a 'threat' has been manufactured, putting into action the type of conspiracy theory that alleged US government involvement in 9/11. In the film a virus is released killing many members of the population and the blame is placed on Muslim extremists, with an extreme Christian fundamentalist party, Norsefire, taking power in the resulting climate of fear. Once in power, Norsefire tightens repression against those who do not fit its particular vision of England. In particular we see the consequences of homophobia when it becomes government policy, as homosexuals are rounded up along with political opponents to be 're-educated'.

Into this arena steps V who is working towards 'waking up' the population as to what they have allowed to happen in their name with his campaign of terrorist bombings. The political and ethical questions raised by V's mission are almost too many for one film to contain as familiar image after familiar image piles on top of each other. There are references to concentration camps, Abu Ghraib, Big Brother-style surveillance, state media control and spin, 'America's war', riot police, a leader's portrait in every house, corrupted priesthood, water boarding, collateral damage, redaction, rendition – an almost exhausting parade of recognisably contemporary fears and representations of the abuse of power, only depicting a more extreme near future dystopia.

It was not just the content of the film that proved to be controversial as events from the real world overtook its release. It was due to be released with the tagline 'Remember, remember the 5th of November' on November 5 2005. However, the very real terrorist bombings in London of 7 July 2005 gave the distributor pause for thought and the release date was moved back five months into 2006 so as to avoid charges of insensitivity in releasing a film depicting terrorist attacks on London so soon after a real event.

Ideology

Underneath all the themes both 'private' and 'public' we find the typical ideology that can be found in many Superhero movies. 'Freedom Forever' was one of the promotional taglines used, and it is this ideology that is the foundation of much of the film. As it is a film based on a British graphic novel its treatment of ideas about freedom are different from those found in American Superhero movies. American Superheroes tend to act in a clearly moral way (Batman being at times an exception) in defending freedom as a value that is shared by both government and the individual. When there is a clash between an individual's freedom to act and the rule of law circumstances usually give them 'a pass' and all ends well. V is neither the morally certain Captain America or Superman, nor the conflicted Spider-Man, nor even the relentless vigilante The Punisher. He knows he is a terrorist and makes no apology for this status; he is in conflict with anyone who cannot see that there is something wrong with the Norsefire government. This is probably why his death is as close to a happy ending as it is possible to get, as there is no more a place for V in this new future than there would be for any of his enemies. In *V For Vendetta* freedom exacts a high, morally grey, price in many different ways for individual and state alike.

Summary

V is a terrorist as well as a Superhero and it is the things we vaguely recognise from our own world that get us thinking about the ideas behind the film. As V proclaims to one of his enemies: 'Beneath this mask there is more than flesh. Beneath this mask there is an idea... and ideas are bullet proof.'

Chapter 8 Characters and Stars

In this chapter we will cover:

- Who and what are characters in the Superhero movie?
- How important are stars and how are they used?
- Representation.

Close up: the exam

Whenever you watch something try to think if any of the characters are similar to ones you have seen in other films. Who are the stars? Could any other actors take their part? If so, who?

Who was that masked man?

17: *Superman Returns*

Characters

In a previous chapter we established that:

A Superhero movie can be defined as a movie that centres on individuals who use their powers for public rather than personal good, often against an enemy who uses their powers for personal rather than public good. Most are sourced from comic books.

That largely takes care of the hero, the powers, the secret identity, the 'mission' and so forth. When characters in a particular genre are so similar they are sometimes labelled **stereotypes** and/or **archetypes**. What do these terms mean? Here are the definitions we used in earlier chapters:

Stereotype: a simplified representation of a person or group of people, repeatedly used so it becomes seen as the norm.

Archetype: an instantly recognisable representation of a character that has been in use for a very long time.

This raises two questions: what is the difference between the two, and how do they apply to the Superhero movie?

In the case of the stereotype it usually has more negative associations as a form of 'storytelling laziness', often being offensive to the person or group involved. Hollywood films are littered with these narrative shortcuts: black jive-talking drug dealers, dumb blondes, rude Frenchmen, villainous Brits, the list is almost endless. What we also need to recognise is that *positive* stereotypes can be equally misleading: the blond, blue-eyed hero, the tenacious single mother and so forth. As we think about the Superhero movie we need to be aware of the 'stereotype trap' and ask ourselves, is this character a stereotype or are they more complex than this? Plus, is it possible that some characters (usually minor ones) are stereotypes because there is no time for them to be anything else and are they balanced out by less clichéd characters elsewhere in the film?

Close up: the classroom

Using one or more Superhero movies:

- Make a list of the stereotypes you have seen.
- Why have they been used?
- How could the characters been improved?

The archetype is usually viewed with less suspicion; in some ways we greet them like an old friend be they hero or villain. Their familiarity helps us to recognise them and understand what is going on. Again we must be careful here; if a character is to be considered an archetype then they should have readily recognisable traits. Yes, the Superhero movie has them. In *Superman II* General Zod is an archetypal villain from his plans of world conquest through his enmity towards Superman right down to his villainous moustache. In opposition to this, many modern Superheroes (thanks to Stan Lee) have flaws and problems that we recognise in ourselves. In some ways this has become a comic book archetype but not a general one that can be recognised in other and older forms.

Close up: the classroom

Using one or more Superhero movies:

- Make a list of the archetypes you have seen.
- Why have they been used?
- Try to come up with their equivalent from films from other genres.

Key terms

Representation:
How people, groups, races or religions are portrayed on-screen. The ideas and assumptions about who and what they are that are generally used.

Any discussion of character types inevitably brings us back to the issue of **representation** and how groups and individuals are portrayed on-screen. The Superhero movie is as good at this, and perhaps marginally better, than the average Hollywood blockbuster. Examples of this can be found in *Daredevil* where the Superhero is blind, and this blindness is referenced in practical ways throughout the film as we get insights into how Matt Murdock manages his everyday life. Indeed, through the use of his superpower we avoid the blind person movie cliché of them feeling people's faces. When Stan Lee came up with this notion of a physical rather than emotional or mental flaw he was concerned it may offend or upset the blind community. This fear was unfounded as he received many letters of support from blind people saying it was great to have a blind superhero. The issue of disability is also considered in an interesting way, as at times in many cases in the Superhero genre the superpower is viewed as a disability. This emphasises that differing abilities are just this – differences – rather than making them 'better' or 'worse' people. In *X-Men*, Rogue has a superpower, but her ability to absorb people's powers means she cannot touch anyone for the rest of her life, at one point even considering 'the cure' to become 'normal' again.

There are other less conventional representations to be found in *Daredevil*. The white crime lord of the comics is replaced by a black actor in the film (although this is arguably merely swapping stereotypes) and the main female character of Elektra is strong and at least Daredevil's equal, the character earning her own sequel in *Elektra* (2005).

It is largely up to you to decide between archetype and stereotype, fair or unfair representation, and argue the case when it comes to the following list and the examples of those typical characters to be found in Superhero movies.

18: *Daredevil*: Positive representations – blind crime fighter and strong independent woman; but what about the black crime lord and mad Irishman?

Characters

Below is a list of some of the typical characters that appear in Superhero movies. Although most will appear here, there will be others.

The hero

The straightforward hero, initially reluctant at times, usually male; the one with the super powers or their equivalent. They usually begin the story as an ordinary person (without powers). They will have struggles to adapt to their new situation, often complicated by their secret / dual identity, and may have unresolved issues (often parental) from the past. Their development will be a central feature of the film, particularly the first of a franchise. They are sometimes played by a star, but more often by either an unknown or somebody famous for their acting ability. For example, Christopher Reeve was unknown until cast as Superman, and Christian Bale was (and is) a respected actor but not a star when cast as Batman.

The villain

The main opposition to the hero. They will have their own super power that they use to further their evil schemes. It may be that they are the 'evil genius' type, such as Lex Luthor, who sees the hero as the main obstacle to their schemes. Often arrogant and disdainful of normal humanity, they pursue their plans by any means necessary, even when their motives may come from an understandable place. For example, in *X-Men*, Magneto's deep distrust of non-mutant kind is born of his childhood experience at the hands of the Nazis. Their sanity may be often called into question, as in the case of Dr Octopus in *Spider-Man 2*, who becomes unbalanced when obsessed by his work, saving New York only when he realises what he has become, not wanting to 'die a monster'.

The side swapper, or the hero turned villain / the villain turned hero

Super villains can be someone who tried being a hero and changed sides. In *X2: X-Men United* Pyro begins the film as a rebellious member of Xavier's school for the gifted but is seduced by Magneto and his ideas about mutant supremacy. Some heroes start their career as villains and redeem themselves by taking up the cause of good. In *Fantastic Four: Rise of the Silver Surfer*, the Silver Surfer begins life as the unfeeling Herald of Galactus but his contact with humanity persuades him to turn against his all powerful master to help save Earth. This transformation from hero to villain or villain to hero is much more common in the comic books where there is more narrative space for this kind of 'experimentation'.

The bad guys

The lower rank of criminal that heroes test themselves against: common thieves, muggers, bank robbers and so on. In a normal context these would be the most violent and dangerous of criminals but are rendered powerless by the Superhero's meta-human abilities. Even a hugely powerful mafia style crime lord like Carmine Falcone in *Batman Begins* is easy prey for the Scarecrow. In *The Dark Knight*, all of the gang bosses are united by their fear of Batman and his one-man war on their activities.

The strong or modern professional woman

They are usually a 'career girl' type and have been ever-present since Lois Lane appeared in *Superman* way back in 1978. They could be broadly described as positive female role models or representations. The scientist Betty Ross in *The Hulk*, the capable executive Pepper Potts in *Iron Man* and the dedicated crusading lawyer Rachel Dawes in *Batman Begins* and *The Dark Knight* are examples of these. What is less positive, however, is that they are often reduced to the status of a 'damsel in distress' during the course of the movie, which undermines their strength somewhat. They will quite often double up as the love interest for the hero which again raises some questions over the role of apparently modern women in the superhero narrative.

The mentor

A Superhero will often have somebody he turns to for guidance or inspiration who acts as a mentor, particularly during their development or in times of doubt and difficulty. Sometimes they will share the secret of their true identity, sometimes not. Batman has Alfred, Superman his father Jor-El, Spider-Man his Uncle Ben, The X-Men Professor X and so on.

Supporters

Closely related to the mentor are the Superhero's supporters. These are the people that have an important role in the hero's mission; again sometimes they will know the hero's true identity, sometimes not. For example, Lucius Fox and Police Commissioner Jim Gordon are close supporters of Batman, and Foggy Nelson and Ben Urich are close supporters of Daredevil.

Authority figures

These are often representations of the more conventional controlling side of society. Whilst not being an out-and-out enemy of the hero they will often persecute them for their own reasons. They become a 'thorn in the side' of the hero but as they are not criminals the hero tolerates their interference. Daily Bugle editor J Jonah Jameson in the *Spider-Man* films, Senator Kelly in the *X-Men* movies and General Ross in *The Hulk* are all examples of this type of character.

19: Is it an archetype? The public, just waiting to be saved?

The public

Whilst not, strictly speaking, an individual 'character' in their own right they do perform several important roles in the different guises they appear in throughout Superhero movies. As individuals they provide the victims for the hero to protect and rescue and will often be interviewed 'vox pop'-style for their opinions as to whether the hero is a force for good or for bad. Linked to this is their role collectively as the most important judge of the hero: public opinion is often a vital element in justifying a hero's actions, and it is not always positive. *Hancock* is a good example of this, as the eponymous hero is reviled for his careless and dangerous 'acts of heroism' until, with the help of a grateful PR man, he redeems his public image.

Close up: the classroom

How did I do?

- Did I miss anybody out?
- What do you think of this list?
- Would you make it longer or shorter? How and why?

Stars

The Superhero Movie has both a conventional and an unconventional approach to the casting of the main parts in its films. **Stars** are expensive and in traditional blockbusters this cost is justified by their use as a USP, a marketing tool to bring in a large audience. Increasingly in the modern blockbuster, however, the really big budgetary expense is reserved for the visual effects that are the modern 'star' of the blockbuster. The principal cast members are often relative unknowns who can be turned into stars by appearing alongside the expensive special effects – how many people had heard of Shia Labeouf until he stood next to Optimus Prime in *Transformers*? The same could be said of Tobey Maguire who was a well known actor before *Spider-Man* but could be considered a star thereafter.

Conventionally a star is cast so that they can bring a large audience to the movie. Audiences identify with the 'big' stars and usually have positive expectations based on the star's previous films. The distributor can then use their presence to sell the film to the public as they know people will be open to going to see something in which they feature.

Superhero movies have featured stars in this way; the producers of *Superman* cast both Marlon Brando and Gene Hackman, two of the most respected American film actors of their generation, to bring some 'respectability' to a project that may have been received less than seriously otherwise. Blade (Wesley Snipes), Daredevil (Ben Affleck), Ghost Rider (Nicholas Cage) and particularly Hancock (Will Smith) can be seen as **star vehicles** for the lead actors. The presence of Snipes, Affleck, Cage and Smith respectively generated audience interest in the films, especially Will Smith who in the Noughties emerged as the world's biggest male star. In the case of Cage and Affleck, it might be said their movies could be considered 'fan vehicles' as both were self-confessed comic book fans of long standing. Cage's name had been attached to many Superhero projects (including the *Superman* re-boot) until he finally landed the lead in Ghost Rider, doubling his tally with his appearance as Big Daddy in *Kick-Ass*.

When a producer signs up a big star their 'sellability' does come with a large price tag and this cost is the main reason why many Superhero movies are cast less conventionally than some other blockbusters.

Superhero movies have developed, and are to an extent dependent upon, **visual effects**. Until the emergence in the 1990s of computer generated imagery – **CGI** – the Superhero movie was very hard to realise in a 'realistic' way. These effects continue to be very expensive and even blockbusters have a finite budget so choices have to be made. Increasingly (and not just in Superhero movies) it is the special/visual effects that is the '**star**', the thing that will sell it to the wider audience.

Key terms

Star: An actor who has their own audience beyond the parts they play. Their presence in a film may guarantee a good sized audience.

Key terms

Star vehicle: A film marketed and made to 'show off' the qualities that made the particular star attractive to their target audience.

Key terms

Visual effects: Images created in post-production using computer technology often referred to as CGI (computer generated imagery).

Key terms

Special effects: Those traditional physical effects such as stunts and explosions. Often said to be done 'in camera'.

This has been true since the very beginning, the first *Superman* film's tagline being, as noted above, 'You'll believe a man can fly', a direct reference to its **special effects**. This has continued. Where would Spider-Man be without his web slinging, or the Hulk without his transformation?

There is also at least one other very important reason for casting relative unknowns as the Superhero and it is that a star's existing screen persona could make it difficult for the audience to focus on the character. In casting the original *Superman* the producers considered many stars of the day, including Robert Redford. They decided that the audience may not accept him as Clark Kent and be thinking 'that's Robert Redford flying' rather than 'wow, Superman is actually flying'. The same is true of Spider-Man and Tobey Maguire. Anybody could be in the suit but would we really believe in a big star as an awkward science nerd high-school student? Of course, if a franchise is successful the role will be seen as a 'star-maker' as the actor becomes world famous.

Close up: the classroom

As a group make a list of your favourite modern stars.

- Decide what type of character they would be in a Superhero movie.
- Who would you chose and why?
- What about 'playing against type'?

20: *Hellboy*

Sometimes a director envisages a specific actor for a part and is relying on their appearance and/or personality to make the on-screen personality more convincing. Guillermo Del Toro has said as much in regard to the lead in *Hellboy* and Ron Perlman, who played the role. Similarly, John Favreau fought to cast Robert Downey Jr. as Tony Stark / Iron Man, as when it came to the irresponsible playboy aspect of the character he would be in some way 'playing himself'.

Another casting tradition that has become associated with Superhero movies is that of the cameo and the name check. As already mentioned, Stan Lee has made multiple cameo appearances in the Marvel movies. Other comic book creators have done likewise (both comic author Frank Miller and film director Kevin Smith pop up in *Daredevil* for example). Often the original creators provide the names for minor characters as part homage and part 'in joke' for the fans; for example, the boxers Romita, Miller, Mack, Bendis, the pathologist Kirby and the criminal Quesada are all named after famous contributors to the *Daredevil* comic book.

Close up: the classroom

Listed here are actors considered but not cast for the roles in two Superhero movies:

- *The Fantastic Four*:
  Brendan Fraser (Mr. Fantastic), James Gandolfini (The Thing), Paul Walker (The Human Torch), Kate Bosworth and Rachel McAdams (The Invisible Girl).

- *Batman Begins* (for the role of Batman):
  Joshua Jackson, Billy Crudup, Cillian Murphy, Hugh Dancy, Jake Gyllenhaal.

Using these or researching some alternatives of your own, discuss whether they would have worked.

Close up: the exam

When thinking about characters, try to find the kind that crop up over and over.

- Why is this?

- Does the actual character change very much in Superhero movies of different ages?

- How are you and other people you know represented? Is it fair?

What have we learnt?

In this chapter we have seen that:

- As with all genre films we must acknowledge that certain types of characters will be re-used from movie to movie. This is fine if either we enjoy seeing these types or if a new spin is put on them by either director or actor.

- This is the challenge of genre films, using the 'formula' yet managing to put an individual stamp upon it. In interviews actors will often talk about what sets their performance apart from the other similar roles that have gone before.

- We should also realise that casting is always a 'tricky business' and mis-casting can be a major handicap for a film – especially in the case of a Superhero movie when we may have to balance the fame of the actor with the fame of the character.

Chapter 9 Production

In this chapter we will cover:

- What do we mean by the film industry?
- How financial decisions interact with genre.
- The changing ways we can consume films.
- Censorship and its role in production decisions.

Close up: the classroom

This is a big topic. Always try to relate it back to your own experience.

- What have I seen? Where did I see it? What have I bought? Why?
- Remember you are a member of the film industry's most important audience group. Why?

21: Chris Hemsworth (left) and Stellan Skarsgård (centre) being directed by Kenneth Branagh (right) on the set of *Thor*

Industry and Genre – Franchise and Super-Franchise

Industry and Genre

Key terms

Production: Activities involved in the actual making of the film.

Distribution: Deciding where a film will be shown and publicising it.

Exhibition: Where the film is shown – cinemas of varying types.

The film industry – **production, distribution and exhibition** – is no different from any other business in its need to make money. Profit is needed to keep shareholders happy and ultimately to make more movies.

One of the main reasons we have genres in the first place is that Hollywood saw these as formulas for success, recipes that they could re-use to achieve the financial returns they needed.

It is a common criticism that these movies are 'formulaic', yet financially it is a deliberate strategy to 'recycle'. This recycling of ideas is an attempt to reduce risk and sell a product with a good financial track record. Hollywood feels little pain when accused of a lack of originality if the box-office receipts are high enough. Often the critics forget that this is how this branch of the arts/entertainment industry has always functioned. The remake or re-used narrative is as old as the American film industry itself. Even before the emergence of Hollywood, some stories were remade four times or more if they proved popular enough.

Superhero movies are a good example of this, despite the 11-year gap between *Superman* (1978) and *Batman* (1989) and the subsequent 10 years where there was only the *Batman* franchise to speak of. When we reach 1998 the story is very different. The success of *Blade* and *X-Men* coincided with advances in visual effects that overcame many of the problems associated with bringing superpowers to the screen. After this point the floodgates opened, with many studios investing heavily in this new blockbuster genre.

Key terms

Package: A deal put together by a producer that contains the main elements of a film: a property, director, star(s). They can then 'sell' this package to investors to secure finance.

Aside from the new technology the genre had one other important factor in its favour – the properties upon which the films are based. Superheroes and their comics have been around for decades and many of them have already become big parts of popular culture. This brings with it an audience of fans and a certain amount of recognition from the wider audience. Both these factors make a film easier to sell (more about this in the next chapter) and reduce the risk involved. Superhero movies are expensive to produce and this can make them risky. One way a studio or producer can try to reduce this risk is to make sure recognisable characters are part of their **package**. If an expensive film is to make money it will need every advantage it can get, particularly the 'built in' audience a popular character or characters can bring with them.

Close up: creative work

A package is very similar to a pitch.

- Put together your own dream package. Include a property, star(s), and director.

- Explain to potential investors why you have chosen each element.

- Convince them that your 'blockbuster' package will become a box-office blockbuster success.

Franchise

Films are based on one of two main sources – an **original screenplay** or a pre-existing **property**. The most common is the pre-existing property, mainly as there is such a wide variety that producers are prepared to use – novels, comic books, plays, magazine articles, true stories and, of course, old films.

The 'holy grail' of production in many ways is the successful franchise. If a producer or studio is to launch a successful Superhero franchise then they will have to buy the **film rights** to the comic book. These days, because of recent successes, the rights to a comic book Superhero may be very expensive, but this has not always been the case. During the early 1990s, when the genre was unproven and Marvel was in financial difficulties, famous B-movie producer Roger Corman was able to make a $4 million version of the Fantastic Four which included the rights fee. You may not have seen this version as it remains unreleased, the official reason being that it was made quickly and cheaply in order to retain the rights. Indeed, to this day many of the rights to popular Marvel characters are held by other studios who will keep them while they continue to use the characters in their movies.

What is a 'franchise'?

A franchise is where a film (and its sequels) are part of a larger business entity composed of multiple tie-ins and merchandise licences. These have become more deliberately planned in recent Hollywood history, for example, *Spider-Man*, *Spider-Man 2* and *Spider-Man 3*, with a re-boot due in 2012.

It all starts with the movie. It used to be that producers and studios would wait and see if a film was successful before planning a sequel. This was the case with *Superman*, although they did film the first and much of the second film together. Escalating costs and uncertainty led to some of the material for the second film being used for the first and some of

Key terms

Original Screenplay: A script for a film not based on any other source. An original idea.

Property: Any source of ideas that has been used to create a film.

Film Rights: The legal permission to use another party's copyrighted characters(s) in a film.

Key terms

Franchise: Where a film and its often planned sequels are part of a larger business entity.

Tie-ins: An individual piece of a franchise directly related to the film.

Spin-offs: When a film leads to other related projects, e.g. computer games, TV shows, other films.

the scenes setting up the second being removed. But when the first film was a success, earning over $300m dollars, the producers returned to the footage they had and, with a new director, fashioned a sequel that was quite different from the one originally intended. These changes can be seen as the different versions of the films have subsequently been released on DVD. The franchise yielded two further films until the box office declined to such an extent that the franchise came to an end.

These days there is more planning and focus on a franchise from the start as principal actors are signed up for three or more films to help ensure the series can continue with the recognisable characters in place. These 'sign ups', however, are in the form of options so the studio is not bound to complete the franchise if it is not a success. The cast of the *Fantastic Four* films, for example, were optioned for more films than have been made so far.

Key terms

Conglomerate: A large business made up of many smaller ones.

A successful franchise embraces many more aspects or 'ancillaries' as they are sometimes termed. Often these secondary products will be produced by companies connected to the studios due to the fact that they are owned by the same parent company as part of a larger **conglomerate**. For example, a conglomerate may own a publisher that can put out the book of the film and other publications linked to the franchise. At 20th Century Fox, owned by News Corporation, books stemming from a film may be published by Harper Collins, the publisher owned by News Corp. So a successful franchise can be very important to many parts of the conglomerate.

Where a conglomerate does not have the facilities to produce something, the studios will license the rights for other companies to make the products. Companies not connected with the studio will pay considerable fees (and sometimes a share of their profits) to get in on the act of a successful franchise. These ancillary products are many and there is often a vast range of material available – the two traditional being ones tie-ins and spin-offs. As movie-making becomes more expensive, these are other sources of income a successful franchise can generate.

Close up: the classroom

Try to come up with as many different kinds of property that could be turned into a film.

- Is there anything that cannot be turned into a film?
- What Superheroes are there left out there to turn into movies?
- Which one would you choose and why?
- Include casting suggestions and other ideas about its production you may have.

Tie-ins

A definition: an individual piece of a franchise, designed to cash-in on the interest generated by a film. These take many forms – for example, the book of the film, or, more recently, the computer game of the film.

Tie-ins with movies have been sources of revenue for many decades; traditionally they have taken the form of books, soundtracks and comic books. The books usually took the form of novelisations of the film, although behind-the-scenes publications soon followed. Soundtracks of both the score and the songs used in a movie have been common for a long time. Where the film was aimed at a younger audience a comic book version might be produced under licence by one of the comic book publishers.

Over recent years the scope of the tie-ins has increased considerably to include fast food restaurants, and free promotional DVDs and USB sticks as just a few examples. Wider still in exploiting their property is the spin-off project.

Spin-offs

A definition: when a film leads to other related projects, for example films, computer games, TV shows. Where products that are not directly related to the event of the movie but utilise the characters and / or universe, the scope is even wider and these have in effect 'spun-off' from the main film. Increasingly the term used to describe this is 'cross-platforming', where different media are used to exploit the film. Examples of this could be computer games, TV series and, moving full circle, other films.

22: *Batman: Arkham Asylum* (2009) – Batman and The Joker get to grips with yet another platform.

Most Superhero films have their computer game equivalent, often produced by another part of the business that owns the movie. Spin-off computer games include virtually all of the Superhero movies from the first *Batman* movies through *Blade*, *The X-Men*, *Spider-Man* and *Iron Man*.

An example of a spin-off TV series recently was *Blade* (2006). Often these are short-lived as they lack the impact a movie budget can bring. Sometimes they are more successful than the original film; in the case of the *Stargate* TV franchise (1998-2011) there have so far been four separate TV series spun-off from the ideas set up in the original movie (1994). Spin-off Superhero movies are often attempts to translate the 'universe' concept from the comic book world (more on this later in the chapter); *Elektra* 'spun-off' from *Daredevil*, Wolverine got his own movie as a result of the *X-Men* franchise.

These days the distinction between tie-in and spin-off is rarely made. Most of the products tend to be referred to collectively as **licensing** or **merchandise**. Many experts date the real start of all this to the point where George Lucas demonstrated with his *Star Wars* franchise that these sources of income can be worth even more than the actual movies (20th Century Fox gave him the merchandising **rights** for free as part of an agreement to reduce his fee on the first film). Ever since then films aimed at a similar audience to Superhero movies have usually been accompanied by a deluge of merchandise – for example, on its release there were 92 separate items listed for *Watchmen* on Play.com alone!

Here are a few examples of the merchandise manufactured to tie in to *Watchmen*:

Key terms

Licence: The agreement that allows one company to use another's property. It will involve a fee and/or a profit share.

Merchandise: Products you can buy based on the film, many in number, ranging from toys, through souvenirs through clothing to expensive prop replicas.

Rights: The legal permission that allows one person to use another's ideas.

23: *Watchmen* merchandise

Close up: the classroom

Choose a recent Superhero movie and search a website such as Amazon or Play to see just how many items are available.

- How many were there?
- What was the cheapest?
- What was the most expensive?
- Which did you expect?
- Which didn't you expect?

What does this tell us about the importance of merchandise to a Superhero movie franchise?

Other Sources of Income

The early Superhero movie producers could have only dreamed about the money that the home market generates for the film industry. Once a film leaves the theatres it will earn its producers and distributors more revenue from cable television fees, terrestrial television fees and the all-important DVD release.

DVD and home viewing is probably now as important (if not more so) for most films than the money from theatrical exhibition. These days the film can come out on DVD a matter of weeks after a cinema release (in a few cases simultaneously) and is a vital source of income for the industry, particularly for non-mainstream films that do not find a theatrical distribution deal or a cinema audience. Many people now prefer to watch their films in the comfort and privacy of their own homes – frequently on home cinema systems with ever more sophisticated picture and sound quality. Just think of HDTV and Blu-ray, with 3D TV now an available home option. Downloading and streaming from sites such as iTunes and Netflix is rapidly becoming an important source of revenue.

If a DVD is to be successful then it needs to compete on the shelves with the vast number of other releases each month. An important factor in this is the design (hopefully eye-catching) of your DVD cover. Annotated overleaf are the typical features of a DVD cover:

Technical information and extra content guidance

Main image is colourful and eye-catching and usually based at least in part on the theatrical poster

Title in a style and font designed to stand out

Star names used to sell the DVD, based on their reputations

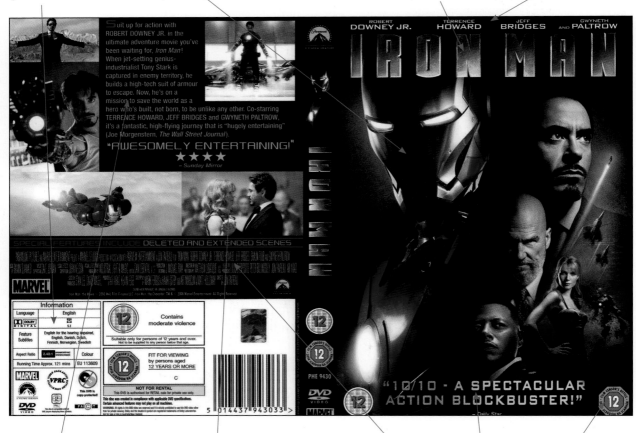

'Blurb' or narrative summary designed to interest the audience and make the film sound enticing enough to buy or rent

Stills from the film show some indicative 'highlights', main characters or moments likely to be of most interest to a potential viewer

Billing Block tells us who are the key cast and crew in the production

Favourable reviews from magazines, newspapers, etc.

Certification as a guide to audience suitability

Key terms

Product Placement: When a film features products and brands prominently in return for a fee or sponsorship.

Generating income is not just about the things that you can sell based on the film. Increasingly we see **product placement** in films. This involves the film featuring products and brands prominently and has become increasingly obvious as production budgets grow and money is required in greater amounts and from wider sources. The company who gets to place its products in a prominent position (and veto its competitors appearing) will have to pay a fee and supply its products to the production for free. The first trailer of *Thor* featured product placement from Dr. Pepper. This follows a series of product placements for the drink in Marvel films, including *Spider Man*, *X-Men* and *Iron Man*. Sponsorship of events surrounding the film (if not the film itself, yet) such as the premiere, may also be a source of income for the producers.

Close up: the classroom

Can you think of any examples of product placement?

- Does this spoil the movie for you? Why?
- Do you think there should be any rules or guidelines controlling product placement?

Despite its role in 'enhancing the cinematic experience' 3D can also be seen as a way of raising further revenue. A significant proportion of the record-breaking $2.8 billion dollars taken by *Avatar* (2009) is down to the higher ticket price we have to pay to see the 3D version. For many years 3D was considered a gimmick or a novelty attraction. But what we consider to be a gimmick can change – early moving pictures were themselves considered a mere novelty item. Many other technical advances such as sound, colour and widescreen were considered as gimmicks initially, as they were developed as responses to competitive threats from other studios or television. This may be about to change with 3D technology, as it seems to be here to stay. With the backing of James Cameron, Steven Spielberg and George Lucas – with even Martin Scorsese championing the new technology – it may become a permanent fixture in our cinemas.

What we can be sure about when it comes to the 'other sources' of income is that studios are both long-practised and imaginative in squeezing as much revenue from their products as is possible.

The 'Super-Franchise'

A potentially new franchise phenomenon is currently moving towards us in the form of the *Avengers* film in 2012. This will unite the characters (and most of the actors) from five previous Marvel Studios films: *The Incredible Hulk*, *Iron Man*, *Iron Man 2*, *Thor* and *Captain America*. This has been a deliberate strategy on the part of Marvel Studios to replicate the Marvel universe concept of the comic books on-screen in its movies.

The idea behind the Marvel universe is very simple, and very effective: all of the characters in all of their comic books exist in the same universe, meaning that anyone of them could pop up in any of the others' comics. DC Comics work the same way and there have even been 'cross-overs' between both universes in the comics (this is a very distant prospect for the films, though). This is very exciting for the fans as their heroes can work together and even clash in an almost endless combination of story possibilities.

We can see the evidence of this strategy being established in Marvel Studios' very first independent production, *Iron Man*. In a short post-credits sequence a figure emerges from the shadows with a proposition for Tony Stark – involvement in 'the Avengers Initiative'. The figure? Nick Fury, Agent of S.H.I.E.L.D (played here by Samuel L. Jackson). All of the Marvel Studios' films have included 'treats for the fans' of this nature to introduce an upcoming movie or establish the S.H.I.E.L.D (Strategic Homeland Intervention, Enforcement and Logistics Division) presence in the Marvel universe. Jackson's cameo has grown in size until he made a fully-fledged appearance in *Iron Man 2*. Jackson has signed an extensive contract with Marvel to portray this role in *nine* movies altogether. This in itself is an interesting twist arising from the fact that Nick Fury as a character was originally a white man and was re-imagined as a character based on Jackson himself in the Marvel Comics 'Ultimates' alternative universe.

All this is getting a bit complicated (another attraction for us nerds) but in simple terms the universe concept links all these franchises together into a 'super-franchise' like no other franchise before it. The nearest equivalent to it is perhaps Kevin Smith's 'View Askew' universe centered on the characters of Jay and Silent Bob. It is no coincidence that Smith is a big comic book fan, has written for Marvel and DC and even named his daughter after the Batman character Harley Quinn.

So far this idea has been successful in at least generating a lot of interest in the Marvel movies. Its actual success will probably depend on the box-office returns of 2011's *Thor* and *Captain America*, two key members of the *Avengers*. So if you ever wondered why some people (me) stayed in their seats at the end of a Marvel movie, they were waiting for that extra 'little treat' to follow after the credits.

24: Comic Con 2010: Avengers assemble! A dream takes form.

Production and Certification

Production considerations will start to overlap with those of the next chapter – distribution and exhibition – now that we are going to consider certification and the Superhero movie.

Censorship or, more properly, classification, has become increasingly important to production decisions over the past three decades or so. In the late 1960s and early 1970s (pre-*Star Wars*), X certificates (now 18 in the UK) were much more common, with *Midnight Cowboy* even winning the Best Picture Academy Award (Oscar) in 1969 despite its X-rating. But as film production has increasingly focused on the 'key demographic' (14–24 year olds and families) getting the 'right' certificate has become vital in ensuring the biggest potential audience for a movie. If the movie is rated 18, half the key demographic and all the children are prevented from going to the cinema to see it.

This is even more significant when we look at the studios' dealings with the **BBFC** when creating Superhero movies. Producers will tailor their movies, apply pressure and exploit the fantasy element to get a 12A or a PG for a Superhero movie. This is further complicated as Superhero comic books have largely been aimed at older teenagers and an increasingly mature audience over recent decades. This can be a problem if you have a massive franchise like *Spider-Man* that in its comic book form can be quite dark in tone and at times extremely violent, but which sells millions of pounds' worth of children's toys.

When a Superhero movie gets a child-friendly certificate it can lead to controversy. Indeed it is often – mistakenly – said that the 12A was invented for *Spider-Man* in 2002. The BBFC itself stated:

> *Spider-Man* had been passed '12' in April 2002, in spite of a request from the distributor for a 'PG'. The reason for the '12' was that the film contained a level of personal violence and a revenge theme that went beyond what was acceptable under the 'PG' Guidelines – 'Moderate violence without detail ... if justified by its setting'.

> The decision proved to be unpopular with the under-12s who had collected the Spider-Man merchandise, toys, lunch-boxes etc., which were specifically marketed at young children. The BBFC received many letters from disappointed children and some surprised

Key terms

BBFC: British Board of Film Classification. The UK industry body responsible for classifying films and advising on the content of these classifications.

parents, questioning the decision. However, the Board defended the '12' decision.

There was also public pressure on some local authorities to issue a local licence for the film with a 'PG' classification, and between 20 and 30 local authorities issued either local 'PG' or 'PG12' certificates with the condition that all under-12s must be accompanied by an adult. (The responsibility for classifying cinema films lies with the local authorities, but in practice these powers are rarely used. The local authorities are, except in exceptional circumstances, happy for the BBFC to carry out the role on their behalf.)

The distributor of *Spider-Man* decided to re-release the film immediately after the introduction of '12A' so that young fans in parts of the country where local authorities had not changed the rating had the chance to see the film at the cinema. The decision to introduce '12A' had nothing to do with *Spider-Man* or the pressure from parents and children who wanted to see the film. The Board had announced its decision to consider changing the category in September 2000 because it recognised that children were growing up faster and that parents were better placed to decide what their children should watch. For the record, the first '12A' film was *The Bourne Identity*.

Source: http://www.sbbfc.co.uk/CaseStudies/Spider-Man

So as we can see studios will now try to get a 12A certificate for their movie rather than a PG, placing the responsibility to check 'consumer advice' firmly with the parent. This has led to further controversy, particularly in the case of the *Batman Begins* sequel, *The Dark Knight*. To quote the BBFC again:

The justification for the 12A certificate was as follows:

The key classification issues noted were violence and threat, though the examining team felt the violence was, in line with '12A' guidelines, both impressionistic and bloodless. Examiners noted some scenes of strong threat when the Joker menaces other, sometimes innocent, characters. The strongest of these include sight of the Joker touching a gangster's mouth with a knife before killing him (off-screen) and a scene in which he presses his blade into Rachel's cheek. Examiners also discussed the film's tone which included some dark and adult moments.

Though these and other scenes in which characters were held hostage or beaten had considerable psychological impact, they contained little in terms of strong detail – thus presenting a dilemma: should the BBFC be classifying what is actually seen, or what is imagined by the viewer?

Of course, this is a clear element of classification already – and is always taken very seriously. There are many examples of films at

'12A' which contain scenes which imply violence far stronger than seen on-screen (such as the torture scene in *Casino Royale*), but by the same token some '18' works are placed at the adult category for events which are not actually seen in detail (such as the ear cutting scene in *Reservoir Dogs*).

In the case of *The Dark Knight* several factors were noted which supported a '12A' certificate. These included the film's comic book style, the appeal of the work to 12–15 year olds, the clear fantasy context and the lack of strong detail, blood or gore.

Source: http://www.sbbfc.co.uk/articles/site/WhySoSerious

In this case as in others the justification for the violence is that it is in a fantasy context (only a comic book, perhaps?). There may be further questions to ask here, as while we are watching a movie it may feel real, perhaps even more so to children. Aside from this it may also be questionable as to whether the BBFC followed its own 12A guidance on 'imitability':

Imitable behaviour

Dangerous behaviour (for example, hanging, suicide and self-harming) should not dwell on detail which could be copied, or appear pain or harm free. Easily accessible weapons should not be glamourised.

Source: BBFC Classification Guidelines 2009

At one point in the film The Joker kills a gangster with a pencil in a sick 'magic trick' joke. Imitable? Easily accessible weapon? We have come a long way since a string of sausages was removed from *Teenage Mutant Ninja Turtles* (1990) because it resembled a set of Nun-chuks.

Was the 12A certificate that helped to sell all those toys the right decision? In terms of the Superhero movie there will always be the need to compromise some properties to appeal to the children's market that the producers clearly believe this genre of movie should be aimed at. One of the few 18 certificate Superhero movies was *Watchmen* and its graphic content was preserved from the original comic and used as a kind of USP in the marketing campaign.

Further detail on the classification rules and decisions is available from the BBFC's very user-friendly website. It is worth a look just find out why your favourite movies got the certificate they did.

Close up: the classroom

Visit the BBFC's website and look up the classification decision of a film of your choice.

- List the certificate and the main reasons for its award.
- Do you agree with the decision? Explain your judgement.
- Why do you think we need the BBFC?

What have we learnt?

In this chapter we have seen that:

- Film production at this level is both complex and expensive. If this expense is to bring returns, and this risk is to be acceptable, studios will often look to the franchise concept to bring some financial stability to their investment. If we are to continue to enjoy movies made on this scale then they will need to be commercially viable, i.e. make a profit.

- If we have to sum up the business motivation behind franchising it would be the oft-sought business idea of synergy. Synergy is often used when, for example, two organisations merge or one buys the other and they hope to work together as a complementary whole. The assumption is the new organisation can maximise what the two were good at and the new business will be a whole greater than the sum of its parts.

- Franchises are designed to work like this in that all the activities will be mutually supporting. All the tie-ins and spin-offs will earn income but they will also generate pre-release 'buzz' or 'noise' about the movie. This leads us into the next chapter as it is distribution and exhibition that are crucially concerned with generating the 'buzz' or 'noise' around a film to try and get people to go and see it.

Chapter 10 Distribution and Exhibition

In this chapter we will cover:

- The marketing of films.
- Different kinds of audiences.
- The importance of audience and its size.

Close up: the exam

This is a big topic. Always try to relate it back to your own experience and behaviour.

- What have I seen? Where did I see it? What have I bought? Why?
- Remember you are a member of the film industry's most important audience group. Do you know what that audience group is?

The how and who of selling a movie

25: Distribution & exhibition: bums on seats

Distribution is the business of actually getting the film from its producers and into the cinemas. Many of the activities most important to a film's commercial success take place at this stage of a film's life.

Exhibition is where the film is shown – cinemas of varying types. There are three main types of cinema in the UK:

Key terms

Distribution: Deciding where a film will be shown and publicising this.

Exhibition: Where the film is shown – cinemas of varying types.

- **Mainstream/Multiplex** – those purpose-built cinemas with five or more screens showing mainly the popular new releases.

- **Independent** – smaller cinemas, often single site or small chains, showing a mix of mainstream and art-house films, often determined by local conditions and demand.

- **Art house** – a cinema that shows mainly foreign or non-mainstream independent films, often considered high-brow or 'art' films.

There will be exceptions to screening policies but the division between mainstream and independent usually remains fairly clear. As we are considering a mainstream genre concerned largely with 'blockbusters' then most of our exploration of exhibition will be focused on the multiplex.

Close up: the classroom

List the cinemas in your local area.

- Are they multiplex, independent or art house? Which have you visited?

- Find out what they are showing. What are the similarities and differences and why?

Key terms

Opening Weekend: The money a film takes in its first weekend of release.

Box Office: The money a film generates in ticket sales. A reference to where people traditionally buy their tickets.

Our main focus in this chapter will be on the more powerful and influential of the two sectors, distribution. The distributor is largely responsible for the marketing of the film to both audiences and the exhibitors. The marketing of a film involves many activities, gimmicks and schemes and just when we think we have seen them all distributors come up with new ones. Whatever activities they decide on they all serve the same end, to get people into the cinema – increasingly for that all important **opening weekend**. Over recent decades the performance of a film has been increasingly judged on the **box-office** returns from its first weekend on release, particularly in the case of a mainstream genre like Superhero movies.

In the case of the Marvel Studios' 'independent' productions, the distribution rights were held by Paramount until very recently. When Disney bought Marvel Studios they began the process of getting back the rights to all Marvel movie properties by buying back the distribution rights to *The Avengers* (2012) and *Iron Man 3* (2013), guaranteeing Paramount at least $115 million. As we can see, the sums of money involved are not small and emphasise the importance of this often 'hidden' sector of the film industry.

The distributor makes its profit by charging the exhibitor a rental fee for the print of the film. The fee for a print can be a flat fee, i.e. a one-off payment. It could also be, more commonly, a percentage of the ticket sales, which is usually at its highest over the first week of release. To make a good profit from a film a cinema will try to show it for as long as possible as often as possible. If you have ever wondered why the popcorn and other 'stuff' is so expensive and why the cinema is so keen on you not bringing in your own food this is part of the reason. In the case of many films, the cinema may even be treating the film as a **loss leader** for its refreshments, from which they keep all the profits. A **print** is a copy of the film shown by the cinema. These are quite expensive to produce, which is the reason why UK cinemas show most films later than American ones, so they can re-use the US prints. It is only the studios behind the biggest budget films, which may be subject to piracy, that can afford a simultaneous global release. This is set to change as the industry is now committed to digital projection, which will mean high quality DVDs and projectors instead of 35mm prints from 2013. Whatever **release pattern** the distributor adopts they will have a marketing strategy for most films.

Key terms

Loss Leader: A product sold at a loss by a business to promote the sale of its other products.

Print: The copy of a film shown in cinemas.

Release Pattern: How often and where a film will be shown. General release is as wide as possible, limited release may only be London or specialist cinemas.

Close up: the classroom

Find the current box office top ten figures.

• Which films earned the most here and abroad?

• Do you think too much importance is put on the box-office performance?

Marketing

Most people associate the term '**marketing**' just with the advertising of things, but in reality it involves a whole range of activities that add up to quite an involved process. The first concern of most marketing strategies is to decide who the target audience is. The mainstream film industry is no different; from the earliest stages of pre-production the studios are concerned that there will be a large and clearly defined audience for its movie. This will simplify the activities later on in the marketing process because if a film has, for example, a clear genre the promotional activities are easier to design with specific people in mind. Also important in this process will be finding a **USP** (unique selling point). This will be something that can be used to get the film to stand out from the rest. It can involve the story, actor, director or property and is sometimes summed up in the tagline, e.g. 'You'll believe a man can fly'. The tagline for the first *Superman* film is drawing on the-then groundbreaking special effects to sell it to a potential audience. Marketing will also

Key terms

Marketing: The process of finding out what people want, developing a product to meet this desire and then selling it to them.

USP: Unique Selling Point. A marketing term for focusing on the feature of your product that sets it apart from its competitors.

involve test screening to make sure the audience likes what it sees; this often results in re-shoots and sometimes altered characters and even endings.

This process, particularly the promotion, can be increasingly complicated and very expensive. The marketing budget for an expensive blockbuster will be several tens of millions of dollars, much more than the production budgets for many other films, sometimes in excess of 50% of the original production budget. Where does this money go? We need to take a deep breath if we are to try and list all the things it pays for. The main ones we are interested in can be divided into three categories: print, broadcast media and the internet.

Print Media

In terms of the print media, the film poster is at the centre of this activity. Posters take many forms and appear in many locations. They could be teaser, one-sheet, UK quad, billboard and bus T. They could appear in cinemas, newspapers, magazines, on billboards, buses and bus shelters; anywhere they will be seen. Trailers appear in cinemas, on the internet and on television and radio. Illustrated here is a selection of typical movie posters and the elements that make up their design:

Teaser:

Strong main image – dramatic, intriguing and summative

Teasers may include a tagline, but their main function is to make people curious by the use of a strong visual image

26: *Iron Man* teaser poster

Date – the nearer the release date, the more specific it will become

Main Poster (one-sheet):

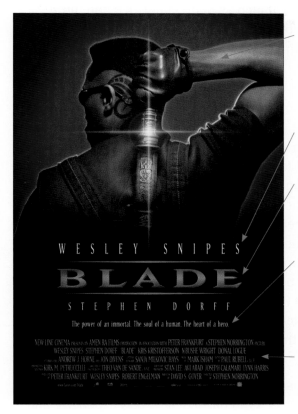

Strong main image – make the potential audience think 'I want to see this movie!'

Star and/or director prominent where he/she is a selling point

Title usually in a bold and dominant position

Tagline – usually designed to arouse curiosity or summarise the film in a dramatic or catchy fashion. Poster may also include critics' quotes from appropriate publications

'Billing Block' – the details of main cast, key production staff and the director. The credits of the film. May also feature the release date, or equivalent (e.g. 'At cinemas everywhere now!')

A UK Quad poster is the landscape version of the portrait American one-sheet. Below are examples of billboards that contain similar elements in a slightly different configuration:

top: 27: *Blade* theatrical poster

middle: 28: *Iron Man 2* billboard

bottom: 29: *Kick-Ass* billboard

The poster is also very important 'point of sale' material to the exhibitor. Many variations will be produced, such as giant stand-ups and large banners often hung from the foyer ceiling. These poster/lobby displays are important in announcing the arrival of the movie and attracting customer attention towards it.

Broadcast Media

At the centre of the marketing activities here is the trailer in its various forms. There may be a sort of teaser trailer, often released quite a way in advance of the movie's opening, as much as a year ahead. There will then be the main trailer (often of varying lengths) for use in the first instance by the exhibitor. When and where to show the trailer can often be an important decision. Some films can be 'trailered' for many weeks before their release to try and build up even more anticipation; some trailers may appear only a few weeks before release. This can sometimes reflect the distributor's confidence in the movie's reception (the longer the trailer the worse the film?). Paradoxically, if the distributor feels the movie is not going to be a big success they will cut back on the marketing as it is expensive.

In addition to the cinema exposure, the distributor will pay for TV and radio 'spots' to publicise the films. TV in particular is very expensive and only those movies that distributors have high expectations of will be advertised on TV. This activity reaches its peak during the week before release, although distributors will sometimes continue with it after this point in an attempt to keep the audience ball rolling.

Key terms

Premiere: The first screening of a film in a country. Typically it will take place in the capital or a major city. The stars will be present and much publicity is generated from their trip down the red carpet.

Advertising is paid-for communication in the media. On a film's release there is also much unpaid-for publicity to be had. PR or public relations work usually involves the stars, directors and others 'doing the rounds' of interviews with all the different media outlets. This is deemed so important that it is a contractual obligation for the people involved in a film. It is very rare indeed for a key player in a movie not to be committed to publicising its release. Other PR 'opportunities' are provided by the studios – there is nothing like a glitzy **premiere** of a film to attract media attention. Most stars understand the importance of these occasions. Tom Cruise, for example, is famous for spending hours on the red carpet with the fans and will even talk to your mum on a mobile phone now and again. When awards season comes around, roughly January to March, the whole PR machine cranks into action as the media is once again full of free publicity for the film industry. By the time the 'big ones', the Oscars, roll around, speculation and coverage is everywhere and can add vital box office to films that are not obvious mainstream successes.

30: Shia LaBeouf, Rosie Huntington-Whiteley and Michael Bay attend the premiere for *Transformers 3: Dark Of The Moon* in Shanghai, China

Another way of trying to get the media interested in featuring a film is the press pack. Studios will send out these 'packs' that include press releases, stills, 'freebies' and all manner of stories and features on the film. Hopefully the journalists will find it useful or interesting and use it in their publication or programme.

Close up: the classroom

Choose a movie trailer and analyse its content. Consider:

- Who it shows and why?

- What it shows and why?

- Does it pose any questions? Why?

- Does it make you want to see the film? Why?

- Do you think it is a fair representation of the film?

Compare it to other Superhero movie trailers. Do they take similar approaches?

Is this linked to genre in any way?

The Internet

In terms of the history of film promotion the internet is a relatively new arrival and its use continues to change and develop. The posting of a website now seems a somewhat old-fashioned approach compared to the use of social network sites and virals.

Websites

Websites are now the basic component of any internet marketing campaign, and studios will encourage feedback from fans and movie-goers in an attempt to build up the pre-release 'buzz' around a film. The basic components of an official website can be found in the following example:

Website functions to give visitors a 'sneak peak'

Release date

Prominent title and main image that link in to print materials

Links to other online material and merchandise

Promotions, competitions and activities generates interest

Film production companies and distributors

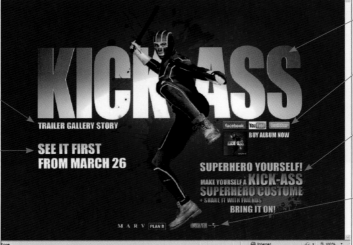

31: *Kick-Ass* official website

Virals

Viral marketing is a new 'spin' on good old fashioned word of mouth. As the internet developed it was not lost on marketing people how quickly rumours spread or the latest 'cool' or interesting bit of video or images were passed around the internet, often becoming overnight phenomena. The production of virals is an attempt to harness this phenomenon to publicise a movie. The term 'viral' is descriptive of how, once 'seeded' online, they spread like a virus from one user to the next, keen to share what they have found. Effective viral marketing can be difficult to get right and studios will often pay specialists to produce their viral campaigns. Virals can include a whole host of both virtual and actual events and activities so can be difficult to coordinate without the right expertise.

In the case of *The Dark Knight* the viral campaign was orchestrated by 42 Entertainment. It was launched many months before the film and was aimed at building up anticipation and filling in the 'narrative gap' between *Batman Begins* and its sequel *The Dark Knight*. They based the viral campaign around the Joker and his catchphrase, 'Why so serious?' This involved many activities, including setting up mock political sites based around the 'I believe in Harvey Dent' campaign slogan. Soon after, a site called 'I believe in Harvey Dent too', mocking the first, appeared to create the impression that a malevolent Joker was actually 'out there'. Materials apparently vandalised by the Joker were also common, scrawling graffiti on posters using his trademark smile to deface images of the other characters. This vandalism approach was so effective that even magazines like *Total Film* adopted it in pre-release articles to suggest this mysterious Joker figure was at work behind the scenes here as well. The slogan 'Why so serious?' would then take the curious to a website that featured trailers and dossiers and other film-related teasers. In addition to this there was a 'Citizens for Batman' website that backed the vigilante's actions and allowed users to interact and view other movie-related materials. These and other websites formed an interlinked patchwork of information and events that kept people interested and, most importantly of all, talking about the forthcoming movie. As the release date drew closer other activities such as scavenger hunts, free screenings and mystery phone calls continued to publicise the movie and add to the narrative as to what had been happening in Gotham City in between the two movies. It is difficult to say how much difference this kind of campaign made to the film's box office but it did become the seventh highest grossing film worldwide. The film was so successful that it influenced the decision made by Warner Bros. to delay the release of their next Harry Potter film, to save a virtually guaranteed high earner for the following year.

Shown below are some of the net-based virals produced for *The Dark Knight*:

32: *The Dark Knight* internet virals

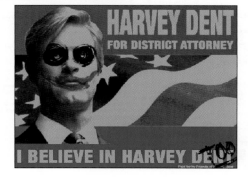

Social Networks

As well as providing an outlet for more 'traditional' internet promotions, social networks are vital to the success of any attempted viral campaign. The official site will have links to many of these kinds of websites but all will include the three most well-known: Facebook, YouTube and Twitter. If we return to *Kick-Ass*, listed below are examples of what was to be found on the social networks it gave links to:

33: YouTube

Trailers and other promotional materials

Other information and opportunities to become involved with the movie

Video content unique to YouTube page with interviews, virals, etc.

User response and interaction

34: Facebook

Links to film details, official and fan photos, official and fan videos, fan reviews and links to related sites

Adverts

Basic information

Fan comment

Links to related sites

Fans

35: Twitter

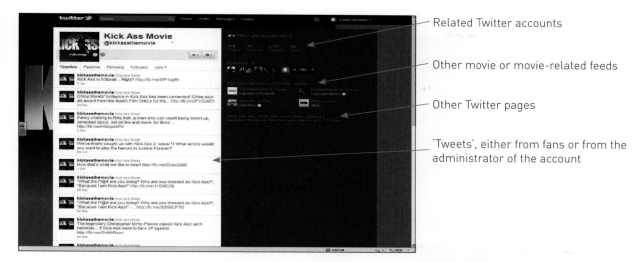

On all of these sites members of the audience, both potential and actual, get to interact with the movie and each other, further building up the interest in the film. As more people sign up to these kinds of websites they will become more and more important in the marketing of films.

Close up: the classroom

Survey:

- How many people in your class use social networking sites and which ones?

- How many have used them to look up or talk about films?

- How many have accessed viral style advertising for films?

- Will this change having studied them?

- Does this tell us anything about the effectiveness of this style of promotion?

Summary

Even though we have considered most of the main kinds of marketing activities, there are more and they are increasing in number all the time. When looking at any promotional activity or material it is important to try and figure out how it works. Ask basic questions such as: how will it interest people in the film? How will it let more people know about the film? You can then use the answers to these questions to devise your own in coursework and examinations. One very important question when it comes to where to promote a film is who will want to see this film? There may be no point in putting up a poster for a blockbuster film in an art-house cinema and this leads us into the final part of this section – the audience.

Close up: the classroom

How many different marketing activities can you think of?

- Compile a class list.
- Which would you use to promote a film?
- Have you ideas for any new ones?

Audience

36: An audience – how do we know what they want?

Key terms

Audience: A group of people with similar tastes and/or characteristics.

So far we have been concerned with what is largely the end result of the marketing process. Before any decisions are made as to how and where a film will be advertised the distributor will work out who it thinks will be interested in the film. This 'who' is what we call an **audience**.

Looking at audience is a bit like looking at genre; it always seems to be more helpful than it might actually be. Like genre, audience is about groups with similar characteristics, only in the case of audience we are talking about groups of people. All this business of putting things in groups is an attempt to make film success easier to understand and predict. Hollywood considers the studying and second-guessing of these groups to be vitally important to the financial success of its movies.

So just who are these groups?

The most common way an audience is defined is by its age. Children, teenager, young adult and adult, are some of the labels used. Often they will have actual ages attached, like 14–19 and so on; usually for the film industry's purposes they will fall in line with the certification boundaries.

Who is the most important?

What Hollywood refers to as the 'key demographic' are the 14–24 year olds (some say it is even narrower than this, Hollywood looking only to 'please' 13–17 year old American teenage boys) as this is the group that visits the cinema the most often and has the most **disposable income**. This goes some way to explain why there are so many 15 and so few 18 certificate films.

An audience's 'status' is also important. Are they single, couples, male, female, families? This will influence the certificate and ultimately the content of a film. Many films will be aimed at an audience that the original source material or property was not in order to secure the biggest potential audience. A film like *Spider-Man* was based on a comic book aimed at older teenagers; the film itself 'needed' family attendance and eventually exploited the new 12A certificate which allows parents to decide for themselves if it is too violent or scary for their children. I wonder how many parents refused to take their children to see *Spider-Man*?

Close up: the classroom

Find out the different categories people in the film industry and business' use to define their audiences / markets / customers.

- Try to think of films that might match each category.

- Can you think of any films that don't really fit any audience category?

- Explain why you think this is.

Whatever categorisation is used, and there are many more in the world of marketing, the idea that a film needs an audience is fundamental to the mainstream film industry. Films will often be denied distribution because the distributor cannot figure out how to sell it and who it can be sold to. The only thing we can really count on is that most films given some sort of distribution (even straight to DVD) will find an audience; only the size is in question.

Many films find audiences away from the **mainstream**. These have their own specialist labels that sometimes fall under the umbrella label of fans or fandom.

Key terms

Disposable Income: The money a person has 'left over' for non-essential spending after paying their living expenses.

Key terms

Mainstream: The general public, the large audience who visits the multiplex and is drawn there by big-budget American productions.

Key terms

Fans: The audience that has a greater level of involvement or interest in a film than the average spectator.

Fans are those people with a specific passion for a film, films, star or genre. Whether these are fans of art-house films, foreign movies, sci-fi or horror they all belong to a loyal, small(er) but significant audience. Their attitudes, practices and spending habits could be the subject of a book on their own. Studying them can be valuable as they demonstrate the kinds of behaviours that are both manipulated and manipulate Hollywood. Individual movie fans can rise in importance like Harry Knowles and his 'Aint it cool news' website, which has allegedly been able to make or break a film. Fans are considered to be a special or specialised audience group.

Of all genres, the Superhero movie may have one of the most important existing fan bases of all. Fans' increased importance to the success of a Superhero movie has been reflected in the rise in importance of the San Diego Comic-Con as a preview venue over recent years. Comic-Con is a comic book convention where fans and creators meet to discuss comics and trade in comics and merchandise. A feature of a convention is the panel event where the creators of a particular comic, show or film answer questions from an audience of fans. Most of the Superhero movies of the last ten years have focused pre-release activities on these kinds of events. The first glimpses of footage and trailers are often tested before this very knowledgeable and demanding audience.

Fans are important in many ways, aside from the fact that many producers, actors and directors claim to be fans (Kenneth Branagh asserted he was a fan of *The Mighty Thor* comic in his youth, long before he was assigned the job of directing the 2011 movie). The fans that buy the tickets can have a massive word of mouth effect on the release of a new film. If a viral can build up a good 'buzz' then 'upsetting' the fans can create an equally powerful negative one. The fans are fans of the comic books first and are very wary of changes being made to the stories they have cherished for years; to ignore them entirely is to play a very dangerous marketing game. This becomes a balancing act as even the most fervent fan realises that you cannot transfer a comic straight to the screen.

Close up: the classroom

Use the internet to find out about a specific group of 'fans. They could be fans of something you like.

- What do you think of their behaviour?
- How much influence do you think they really have?

Conclusion

Overall the film industry needs to be confident that people will want to see a movie. The industry tries to have as clear a picture of this audience as it can from the very outset of pre-production. If an audience is small then it will need to be at least loyal so a smaller budget can be recovered from the film's revenue, even if this is not until after the DVD sales figures come in. Occasionally studios find the 'holy grail' of film production – a small film that captures the imagination and finds a massive mainstream audience. Films like *The Full Monty* (1997) or *The Blair Witch Project* (1999) have managed this. If one 'industrial phenomenon' sums up the magic of movies it is films like this; try as the industry might it cannot turn successes into a re-usable formula. This is good for the audience, for as long as the film-makers are kept guessing about who the audience is and what they want then they will keep trying an ever growing range of ideas. More often than not, though, Hollywood targets and finds audiences large enough to sustain the huge production the blockbuster strategy requires.

Close up: the classroom

Try to find out which films have been most profitable, earning more than their overall budget.

- Does this differ from your work on the box-office receipts for films?
- What does this tell us?

Close up: the exam

The film industry is constantly changing. This section of the book was almost out of date before it was written. Keep an eye out for news stories about films, discuss them in class and try to keep track of them. Always think, how does it affect me? How does it fit in with what I have learned?

What have we learnt?

In this chapter we have seen that:

- As Film Studies students we need to be very aware of the effect decisions by distributors have upon our film choice at the cinema.

- Exhibition is the part of the film industry that we all have first-hand experience of, although perhaps not of all its forms.

- Distribution involves many activities that can add up to a large expense for the distributor so they can be very 'risk averse'. At the moment this works in favour of the Superhero movie as it is popular. If box-office receipts fall for a few films then the distributors may be less keen to take on these expensive projects.

- We also need to remember we are looked at by distributors as a member of an audience. What they may sometimes forget is that it is quite normal to be a member of many different audiences and limiting the types of films they release in cinemas may diminish our choice and their income.

Case Study 3

Iron Man – Sowing The Seeds Of A 'Super-Franchise'

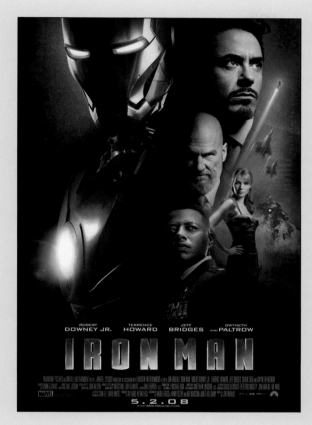

Release date: 2008

Production: Marvel Studios

Producers: Avi Arad, Kevin Feige

Distribution: Paramount Pictures

Director: Jon Favreau

Screenplay: Mark Fergus, Hawk, Ostby

Art Marcum, Matt Holloway, John August

Comic by: Stan Lee, Larry Lieber, Don Heck, Jack Kirby

Publisher: Marvel

Main cast: Robert Downey Jr., Terrence Howard, Jeff Bridges, Gwyneth Paltrow

Music: Ramin Djawadi

Budget: $140 million

Box-office: $585,174,222

Tagline: *Heroes aren't born. They're built.*

Synopsis

Tony Stark is a billionaire playboy industrialist, the very definition of a cynical self-centered capitalist. On a trip to Afghanistan to promote his latest weapons system, his convoy is attacked and he is kidnapped by insurgents, the victim of his own weapons. Waking up and finding himself attached to a car battery to prevent shrapnel from penetrating his heart, he begins a change. Between his life-threatening injury, his return to science and engineering and the conversations with his co-captive, he resolves to be a different man if he can escape, which he does after building the Mark 1 'Iron Man' suit. Back on American soil, at his first press conference he announces the suspension of Stark Industries' weapons production. Obadiah Stane, Stark Industries' CEO and friend of Tony, does not react well and we learn that he plotted Stark's intended demise in the first place. While Stark works on suits 2 and 3, Stane constructs the 'Ironmonger' and they clash noisily in the film's climax. Iron Man is triumphant and Tony Stark announces to the world that he is in fact Iron Man.

Iron Man - The Modern Production, Distribution & Exhibition of a Franchise

Introduction

There are a few reasons why *Iron Man* is an important film for the Superhero genre, both on the creative and business side of the film equation. It was the first step towards 2012's *Avengers* movie which could be establishing the new way of managing a blockbuster franchise.

Production

On the creative side is the successful attempt to create a real-world, believable Superhero. Although not hugely original, both Stark and Iron Man feel as if they *could* be real. Some of this success comes from Stan Lee's original intent - to make a hero out of a character that was at first glance immoral; none could have been more so in the counter culture/ Vietnam War protest 1960s when Iron Man first appeared than a super-rich arms dealer. Director John Favreau and star Robert Downey Jr. were central parts of the production package put together by Marvel Studios' Avi Arad and Kevin Feige who worked together to create 'the world of *Iron Man*'. They succeeded in creating a film that could appeal on different levels from straight Superhero action to a degree of current social and political commentary; a key factor in its critical success.

Perhaps more importantly for the Superhero movie genre was its commercial success. As Marvel Studios' first independent production, its success was key to their ability to proceed with their future projects. It was commercially successful enough for Marvel Studios to absorb the less successful *The Incredible Hulk* later the same year. Even more than this, it successfully seeded interest in the whole 'Marvel Universe' approach to film franchising in including the S.H.I.E.L.D. agent Coulson, a reference to Captain America's shield and an all important post credits sequence featuring Samuel L. Jackson as Nick Fury. In this scene Fury reveals that Iron Man is not the only superhero in the world, and introduces the concept of the 'Avengers Initiative'. Not only does this set up a plot line for *Iron Man 2* (2010) but also puts Marvel Studios on course for their most ambitious project yet, the Avengers movie. In subsequent Marvel Studios films *The Incredible Hulk*, *Iron Man 2*, *Thor* and *Captain America: The First Avenger* (2011), this back-story or 'mythology' increases its presence with the intention of heightening expectation for *The Avengers* film.

As well as this, all the usual sources of income and publicity were drawn upon in the drive towards success. There were **tie-ins** with the comics and other publications such as a movies special edition of the Marvel Figurine part-work collection; and of course the toys ranging from the pocket money playthings through to the expensive collectable maquettes. **Spin-offs** included computer games and re-marketed animated adventures. **Other sources of income** included cable and terrestrial TV revenues and the not inconsiderable DVD sales. **Product placement** we have discussed in the main chapter with both Audi and Dr Pepper featuring prominently as 'commercial partners'.

Distribution

Paramount did not hold back on finance when it came to marketing. Teaser images appeared very early. Advertising across all possible print and broadcast media outlets matched by internet activity was all aimed at creating a feeling of the next big thing. The success of this can be judged by both its **opening weekend** and overall **box office** performance. In the case of *Iron Man*, the marketing should probably be seen as a success in the light of a US opening weekend of $98,618,668 and a total worldwide gross of $585,174,222, more than justifying its $140 million budget.

Exhibition

Iron Man was launched into the multiplex as a typical mainstream action-orientated movie. In terms of its release pattern globally, it was a very tight release schedule, opening in all major markets over a seven day period. Nationally it was showing in 500 of the UK's 770 cinemas, almost a 'saturation' release pattern for the UK, although this is dwarfed by the 4,154 theaters that were showing it on its US opening weekend. Whichever measure one chooses, we can see that between them, Marvel and Paramount made every effort to ensure what many consider to be a B list comic book character made an A list splash in the cinemas.

Summary

Will the super-franchise/Marvel cinematic universe work? Well, only the box-office will tell. The signs so far are good for Marvel: *Iron Man 2* took more money than *Iron Man* and both *Thor* and *Captain American* have proved to be solid commercial successes. If Marvel can pull it off, fans can perhaps dream that in partnership with Disney, there may come a day when all the comic book universe characters are united in the cinematic universe. Now that really would be a super super-franchise!

Part 3 Exploring Film Outside Hollywood

In this part you will learn:

- The differences and similarities between films made in mainstream Hollywood and those made in other parts of the world.

- The social and historical context of a selection of films you can study for this topic.

- The characters and narratives of these films.

- The themes and issues raised in these films.

- The ways in which people, places, events and issues are represented.

- The organisations which produce the films and the audiences who respond to them.

- Your own response to the film and the forms in which this critical response may be expressed.

1: It's a big world out there (clockwise from top left: *The Devil's Backbone*, *The Boy in the Striped Pyjamas*, *Persepolis*, *Rabbit-Proof Fence*, *Ratcatcher*, *Tsotsi*)

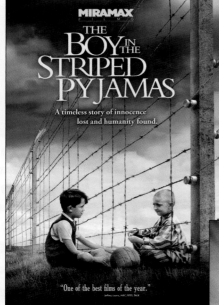

2: Film posters from Hollywood and around the world

Close up: the classroom

Look carefully at the three film posters above.

- Which is the Hollywood film, which is the Australian film and which is the British film?

- What kinds of clues do the covers contain to help you identify their country of origin?

- What kinds of expectations are set up through the choice of images, the titles, genre or stars?

- Which film would you prefer to see? Why?

Given the choice of films above, you would probably prefer to watch the film made in Hollywood. There may be several reasons why. We often choose our films according to their genre, director or stars. Perhaps it's the prospect of having to read subtitles that puts us off watching films in other languages, or we may not have heard of the director or stars. Equally, they may not have had access to the big budgets that typify Hollywood 'blockbusters' and consequently it is unlikely that they will feature the special effects that underpin the spectacle of, for example, the Superhero film. So, we usually base our viewing choices on what we already know and like. We don't want to be disappointed so we pick familiar films from a specific genre, featuring our favourite (often 'A' list) stars or by a director that we really admire. We like the dialogue to be in our own language and a badly dubbed film somehow spoils our overall enjoyment of the cinema experience.

When we come to a film cold we all have a set of expectations. Some of the films you will study for this course, especially for the genre paper, have been made in Hollywood. Often when we think 'cinema', we automatically think 'Hollywood' and then we compare other kinds of cinema to it.

Close up: the classroom

Search the internet for the programme at your nearest multiplex cinema.

- How many films are American? How many are from other countries?

- Look for one Hollywood film and one that was made outside Hollywood on www.imdb.com. What are the films' titles? Who do they star? What are the names of the two directors?

- Now compare the production costs of each film. Which is the most expensive – and why?

- What are the major differences between films made in Hollywood and those made outside Hollywood?

Often when we consider the films made in other countries, we assume that the films are somehow quite different from Hollywood cinema. However, this is not necessarily the case. Although you may already have noticed differences in terms of budgets, stars, directors, style, or settings, most film-makers in every country want to reach as wide an audience as possible, so there are bound to be similarities.

The films you'll be studying for this part of the course were all made outside Hollywood, sometimes produced with finance from more than one country. They are set in several different parts of the world and will give you an insight into those countries and, in many cases, their past:

Key terms

'A' List: The list of stars that are currently attracting the highest salaries and most prestigious film deals.

Dialogue: Conversations between characters.

FILM	SET
Amélie	France, the late 90s
Ratcatcher	Scotland, the mid 70s
Tsotsi	South Africa, the early 60s
The Devil's Backbone	Spain, the 30s
Yasmin	England, the early 00s
Bend It Like Beckham	England, the early 00s
The Boy in the Striped Pyjamas	Germany and German-occupied Poland, 1942-44
Rabbit-Proof Fence	Australia, the 30s
The Wave	Germany, the late 00s
Persepolis	Iran, late 70s and 80s

These films have been chosen because we think you may never have seen them before but also because they are really enjoyable. Some of them contain amazing performances by 'unknown' actors or non-professional actors whose own life experiences may be quite like those of the characters they are playing. The storylines may be funny, sad, exciting or thought-provoking. We hope you will learn something new about the people and places that are featured in the films. Some of the settings may be unfamiliar but the problems or situations which face the characters are not. *Rabbit-Proof Fence*, *The Boy in the Striped Pyjamas*, *The Devil's Backbone* and *Persepolis* are set in specific social and historical contexts – 1930s Australia, Germany during the Second World War, the Spanish Civil War and Iran in the late 1970s and 1980s, respectively – but each of those films explores the events on which they're based through the eyes of a young person. *Bend It Like Beckham*, *Yasmin* and *The Wave* examine the effects of prejudice and living within a fast-changing world. All of the films foreground the experience of young people growing up. All explore what we call 'universal themes' – situations and problems that affect us all at certain points in our lives.

The films in this section are all challenging in different ways, sometimes challenging our expectations about a particular culture or place, sometimes deliberately setting out to challenge stereotypical representations. Whichever film you choose to study, you will need to analyse key sequences closely, beginning with the opening sequence. The work you have already completed on the 'macro' and 'micro' elements of film language will help you to explore how the central characters, specific themes and issues as well as the 'universal' themes mentioned above are represented in your chosen film.

Case Study 1
The Boy in the Striped Pyjamas

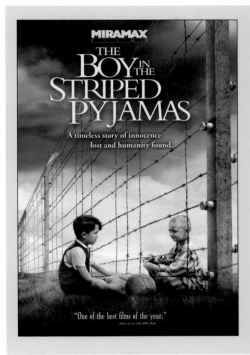

Country: UK/USA

Production Year: 2008

Director: Mark Herman

Certificate: 12A

Main Awards:

British Independent Film Awards: Best Actress Vera Farmiga

Chicago Internatinal Film Festival: Audience choice award

Nominations:

Best Director (British Independent Film Awards)

Best European Film (Spanish Goya Prize)

In this section we will:

- Find out about the time and place in which the film is set.
- Focus upon the key themes and issues within the film.
- Explore the ways in which the 'micro' and 'macro' elements of film language are used to communicate ideas.

Synopsis

Nine year old Bruno lives with his mother, father and older sister Gretel in a large, comfortable house located in the centre of Berlin, Germany. His father is an SS Commandant in the army. When the Second World War begins the family relocates to the countryside where his father is assigned to take command of a prison camp. Later, whilst exploring the area outside his garden, Bruno meets another boy, named Shmuel, strangely dressed in striped pyjamas, who lives behind a wire fence. Bruno knows nothing of the Final Solution and the Holocaust but soon finds out that he is not permitted to befriend Shmuel, as he is a Jew. The friendship takes him from innocence to revelation and his desire to explore the world around him ultimately leads to tragedy.

Close up: the classroom

You may have studied the Second World War in your Year 9 History classes. In pairs answer the following questions. Share your answers with the rest of the class.

- What do you understand by the term Holocaust?
- What was 'The Final Solution'?
- Who was responsible for these policies and why were they developed?

Introduction

The Boy in the Striped Pyjamas is a film based on a novel written in 2006 by the Irish writer John Boyne. The novel has been translated into over 30 different languages and has been read by people across the world. Clearly the themes and issues raised in this story have a universal appeal and relevance. Mark Herman, the film's director, has directed a number of British films, including the very successful *Brassed Off* (1996) and *Little Voice* (1998).

Although the story is fictional, it is based on real events in our world history. It takes place during the Second World War and is initially set in Berlin where Bruno and his family live. However, the major part of the narrative unfolds just across the border of German-occupied Poland, in a place called Auschwitz. Between 1942 and 1945 at least four million people were sent to Auschwitz and although both the film and novel do not give their audiences specific dates, it seems clear from the historical events that are featured that the 'action' takes place sometime between 1942–1944.

The Boy in the Striped Pyjamas is the story of the friendship between Bruno, the son of the Commandant of a concentration camp and Shmuel, a young Jewish boy who is imprisoned in the camp. It is set against one of the most terrible events in human history. Although the children don't realise it, they are experiencing **genocide** unfold first-hand, and Bruno's father is the man giving the orders. In the film, members of Bruno's family and nation describe Shmuel and his people as sub-human, and while the story is a **fable**, it is based upon a time when the **Nazis** acted on such a belief.

The Nazis' attempt to wipe out the Jewish race is often known as the **Holocaust**. Over 6 million people, a large number of them Jews, were killed in the death camps set up throughout Nazi-occupied eastern Europe. Auschwitz, in today's Poland and the largest of the camps built

Key terms

Genocide: The deliberate extermination of a people or nation.

Holocaust: The name given to the Nazis' attempt to wipe out the Jewish race.

The Final Solution: The plan to kill every Jew in Europe.

Fable: A fictional story which contains some kind of moral message.

Nazis: Germany's right-wing National Socialist Party, led by Adolf Hitler.

to kill people, was built after Hitler met with leading Nazis in January 1942. By this time, many European countries were under German rule. This gave Hitler the opportunity to 'cleanse' Germany and other countries under his control of all the people he hated – the mentally impaired, gypsies, homosexuals, political opponents and especially the Jews. The decision to eliminate these people was called '**The Final Solution**' and it is estimated that 11 million people were 'exterminated' – mainly in Auschwitz and the five other major death camps that had been especially built for this purpose.

Because the Holocaust was one of the most terrible events in world history, readers and film audiences bring knowledge and understanding of the boys' respective situations that the characters themselves do not have. This knowledge makes the story even more powerful, because we know the terrible danger that both boys face, and we are forced to witness the tragic consequences of their forbidden relationship.

Themes and Issues

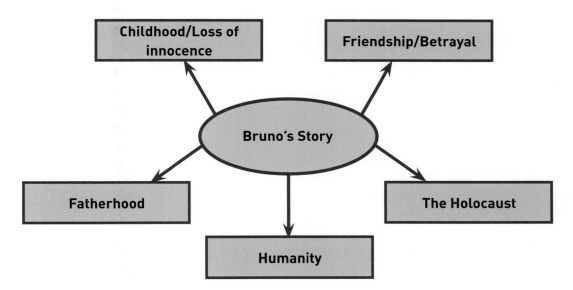

Childhood/Loss of Innocence

As with all the focus films included in the Films Made Outside Hollywood section of the specification, this film's narrative revolves around a young person and his experience of the environment in which he is growing up. One of the major themes in *The Boy in the Striped Pyjamas* is childhood and the loss of innocence. The audience may bring varying amounts of foreknowledge to the film; most will know something about the Holocaust. In the opening sequence Bruno may be lost in an imaginary world of fighter aeroplanes, machine guns and soldiers, where nobody is really hurt and there are no real people to hate, but the audience

3: A world of childhood innocence?

knows differently. He may be unaware of the swastika flags hanging from the large buildings, the uniformed officers and Gestapo drinking coffee in the square below, the Jewish occupants of the crowded tenement buildings being herded onto open trucks, but we are not.

'Childhood is measured by sounds and smells and sights, before the dark hour of reason grows.' John Betjamin

Close up: the classroom

- How does poet John Betjamin's metaphor above foreshadow (gives us clues to) what the film might be about?

Watch the opening sequence of the film from 01.00 – 05.24. Then answer the following questions:

- How is Bruno's innocence about what is happening in Berlin shown?
- How is sound used to extend this theme of innocence?
- What do you learn about Gretel, mother and father and the family's life style in this sequence?
- How are these first impressions created?

Key terms

Swastika: The symbol of Nazi Germany.

The opening sequence is very important both in terms of establishing major themes and allowing the audience to learn about characters. Bruno is clearly shown as the central character. The film language underlines his carefree existence in Berlin and the fact that he is totally unaware of what is going on in the world around him. The opening shot is an extreme close-up of the folds of a fluttering red, black and white flag, which blows back to reveal a large square overhung with other huge flags containing black **swastikas**. Bruno and his friends can just be seen entering the square in this long shot. The streets of Berlin are packed with people, soldiers clamber onto trucks, they stand guard in front of big buildings, officers alight from shiny, black sedans, armed troops use Alsatians to round up the people from tenement buildings and herd them into trucks. Bruno does not notice any of these things. He is a child enjoying playtime with his friends, safe in a comfortable home with a happy family; but his life is about to change and perhaps not for the better.

Close up: the classroom

Watch the sequence from 05.24 to 09.50

- What do we learn about grandmother's attitude to her son's new promotion?

- What is the reaction of the rest of the family to his new role?

- Consider the use of the **sound bridge** at the end of the party and the following morning. Why is it used? What effect does the slowing down of the song have?

- Watch the sequence once more, make notes and write a short analysis of the ways in which sound and mise-en-scène introduce the themes of childhood and innocence in the opening sequence.

Key terms

Sound Bridge: When a scene begins with the carry-over sound from the previous scene before the new sound begins.

The song 'Wish me luck as you wave me goodbye' bridges the end of the party held to celebrate father's promotion to Commandant and Bruno's last game with his friends on the upstairs landing of his Berlin home. He descends the stairs in response to his mother's call for him to leave. He finds his house stripped of furniture and guests and he is about to begin a journey that involves leaving safety, security and, ultimately, his childhood and innocence behind.

Mise-en-scène is important in signalling these changes. The large, comfortable home situated in a Berlin street alongside other equally grand houses, with its comfortable furnishings, warm polished wood, leafy flower-filled garden and open access, is left behind. The security it offered Bruno has also vanished. His family arrive at the forbidding iron gates of an isolated, bleak, grey concrete house. Its nearest neighbour is the death camp that father has come to take charge of. The huge, locked iron gates open onto a hard gravel drive; the heavy front doors lead to an equally bleak interior with a concrete staircase. The house is already occupied by other soldiers and father's office is forbidden to the rest of the family. The bedrooms are dark with small windows situated so high in the walls that Bruno has to stand on furniture in order to see out of them. The wallpaper in Bruno's room with its stripes and arrow-like patterns creates a prison-like feeling. Its harsh lines echo the stripes on the prison uniforms worn by the Jews trapped behind the wire fence, which can just be glimpsed through Bruno's high window.

The act of moving from Berlin to Auschwitz is shown as vitally important in terms of the film's narrative. It signals father's willingness to play his part in the **Final Solution**. It signals the breakdown of relationships within the family, secrets, lies, betrayal and the eventual loss of innocence in the most tragic, shocking circumstances.

Friendship and Betrayal

Friendship is another important theme established early in the narrative. One of the main reasons that Bruno does not want to leave Berlin is because he doesn't want to be parted from his friends. In the opening sequence we see him running through the streets of Berlin with them; they run after his car shouting their goodbyes as he leaves Berlin for his new life in Auschwitz. Bruno cannot settle in his new home because he is isolated, there are no neighbours and school is replaced by a tutor who comes to the house. Herr Liszt further restricts Bruno's world by banning adventure books, poetry and plays – a Nazi education concentrates on a particular view of history, one in which Germany is seen as all powerful and its enemies as 'vermin'.

Bruno's sister, Gretel, is not interested in playing with him; she has reached the age when she is no longer interested in 'childish things'. She abandons her collection of dolls and replaces them with posters extolling the virtues of belonging to the Hitler Youth Movement. She is attracted to the young Lieutenant Kotler and wants to impress him with her maturity.

Boredom and frustration overwhelm Bruno. Without his friends his world shrinks and he becomes deeply unhappy. Ironically, his innocence about the world around him leads him to forge the most important friendship in the film. Whilst exploring 'forbidden' territory at the back of his house he meets Shmuel. Although the boys are physically divided by the barbed wire fence, they immediately connect emotionally. They have not been corrupted by the adult world, its prejudices, cruelty and hatred; they hardly notice their differences and concentrate on what they have in common. They share the same birthday, both have never known anybody who has the same name as their new-found friend, both love football and chess. Shmuel may know more about the injustices of his situation but he does not burden Bruno with them. Bruno remarks, 'We're like twins' and Shmuel replies, 'A little bit'.

As the friendship grows, Bruno's attitude towards his new home changes; he is aware of the growing rift between his mother and father but is comforted that he now has a friend. He begins to question adult opinions and actions – his limited experience with Pavel and now Shmuel has shown him that Jews are not 'vermin', they are capable of great kindness and can be trusted. On the other hand, his father and Lieutenant Kotler have demonstrated awful cruelty. Bruno and Shmuel's friendship is a key theme. It says much about the prejudices that led to a terrible moment in world history. It also carries an important message for us today about the need to bridge cultural and racial divides if we wish to avoid tragedy and create a more peaceful world.

The Holocaust

Although the Holocaust is a major theme in the film, it is seldom referred to explicitly. Bruno is unaware of the horrors that take place at the end of his garden. Shmuel, too, seems unaware of the real fate of his grandparents and, finally, his father. This atmosphere of secrecy in Germany during the Second World War– a reluctance to mention the unmentionable – has been well documented. Amongst the prisoners in Auschwitz and other death camps, many knew but some only suspected (or feared) what their ultimate fate would be. Many were certain about the function of the 'showers' (gas chambers); some clung to a hope that the rumours they heard were untrue. In the wider world, too, there were suspicions, but until the final liberation of these camps in 1945 the scale of the Holocaust remained largely unknown. In many ways, all these fears and uncertainties were rooted in a Nazi policy of silence. As Heinrich Himmler, the Nazi commander responsible for the Final Solution, chillingly addressed to a group of senior Nazis in 1943:

> **Amongst ourselves we can talk openly about it, though we will never be able to speak a word in public. I am speaking about the extermination of the Jewish people. That is a page of glory in our history that will never be written.**

> **- Heinrich Himmler, speech made to senior Nazis in Poznan, 1943**

The film conveys this atmosphere of secrecy very effectively. Mother clearly must have had her suspicions about the nature of the camp. However, it is not until Lieutenant Kotler, when asked about the smoke coming from the high chimneys, says 'They smell even worse when they burn', that she is finally forced to face up to the full horror of her husband's role. Grandfather appears to believe the **propaganda** films, so obviously made to stifle the suspicions of German people and the rest of the world. It's hard to believe, though, that given Grandmother's attitude and the obvious unhappiness of Bruno's mother, that he too isn't just 'turning a blind eye' to the real purpose of the death camps.

Ironically, it is this atmosphere of secrecy and lies that seals the fate of both boys. Bruno expects the inside of the camp to be as it was shown in the propaganda film he has seen . Shmuel enlists his help to find his father who must be hiding somewhere there. Neither realise the danger. Bruno is driven by his need to repair his friendship after denying it to Kotler; Shmuel wants to find his father and allow his friend the opportunity to finally show him some support.

Key terms

Propaganda: Publicity designed to confirm religious or political beliefs.

Close up: the classroom

View the sequence from DVD Chapter 8 of *The Boy in the Striped Pyjamas* twice. Then answer the following questions.

- What is the importance of the dialogue about the smoke and its smell?
- Why doesn't mother join in the conversation?
- What does father tell Bruno has caused the smell?
- What does this tell you about his attitude towards the Jewish people?
- This sequence highlights one way in which **Anti-Semitism** is spread. What is highlighted? Can you think of any other ways in which these ideas and attitudes are handed down from generation to generation?
- How do you know that Bruno questions what he is being taught?

Key terms

Anti-Semitism: Prejudice against Jews.

Narrative

The Boy in the Striped Pyjamas has been described as a **fable**, a fictional story that contains an important moral message. It does not simply look at the Final Solution and invite the audience to experience the shock and horror of this terrible policy. It can be 'read' on a number of different levels, for example, as a comment on the importance of friendship and loyalty, or an observation on the way that prejudice, fear and hatred can be passed on through the generations.

The extra on your DVD called *Friendship Beyond the Fence* highlights the importance of being sensitive about the ways fact and fiction are combined in this film. Every member of the production team was very clear that they were filming a work of fiction and not a documentary. Nevertheless, as the story draws from history, meticulous care was taken to respect the historical context. Perhaps the most controversial aspect of the story was Shmuel's presence in the concentration camp. It is probably the area where fiction and truth separate the most in this film because the awful fact is that most children arriving in the camps were immediately sent to their deaths. By 1944, particularly in Auschwitz, there were children still surviving, but most were taken straight from the transport into the gas chambers.

Producer David Heyman stressed the reasons for revisiting this terrible event in world history: 'History has a pattern of repeating itself and I think that it's very important that these stories are told, in whatever form and by whomever, as long as the emotional content is real and true.' He also underlined the film's more universal message – the dangers of unquestioning obedience to authority, no matter how appalling the demands of that authority.

Close up: the classroom

Watch *Friendship Beyond the Fence* (DVD extra).

- Note down the reasons why those involved (director, producer, cinematographer, actors, etc.) wanted to make the film.

- What does David Heyman (producer) say is one of the main strengths of the story? Do you agree?

- How important was research in terms of the story and 'look' of the film?

Style – The Look of the Film

It is clear both from watching the film and the DVD extra that the behind-the-scenes creative team (cinematographer Benoit Delhomme, production designer Martin Childs and costume designer Natalie Ward) were committed to bringing authenticity, respect and attention to detail to capture one of the darkest periods in history. Many of the film crew were Hungarians and they were acutely aware that Hungary had supported Germany during both World Wars.

Cinematographer Benoit Delhomme did not want to create a glossy, Hollywood look to the film. He wanted to show awkwardness as well as the beauty: 'Sometimes the frame's a little messy; you've got the head of a character in the foreground, blurred. It's not always very neat.'

The opening scenes in the film feature a **montage** of Bruno and his friends running through the streets pretending to be Messerschmitt airplanes. They, like so many young boys in conflict situations today, are seduced by the 'glamour' of the war and don't fully appreciate its horror. They are on their way home from school and journey through different neighbourhoods. We see wealth and poverty and catch a glimpse of Jewish people being herded onto trucks; the boys, however, are oblivious to the social injustice going on around them.

The concentration camp itself was the result of careful research: the sets for the final scene were based on a famous photograph of the gas chamber at Auschwitz. The design for the fence where Bruno and Shmuel meet was seen as very important. Bruno was to be framed against the leafy greens of the forest, Shmuel against the cold greys and browns of the prison camp.

Key terms

Montage: Series of shots which summarise an action or build a mood.

The story is told through Bruno's eyes and much of the dialogue between the boys was shot from their level so that the audience was 'planted firmly in their world'. The use of hand-held camera at the boys' eye level in the closing minutes places us firmly alongside them in the middle of the panic-stricken crowd.

In many ways this is a 'typical' British film using mainly British actors and employing a **chronological** narrative. One critic, when comparing it to the American family film, put forward the view that it was far more intelligent, far less busy and doesn't condescend to children or families. Certainly it is unusual to make a family film about the Holocaust but *The Boy in the Striped Pyjamas* does so successfully, on the whole. It certainly avoids shock for shock's sake, does not overdramatise – even in the final scene – and is able to portray a story of friendship with a degree of realism and truth.

Key terms

Chronological: Arranged in the order of time.

Representation

One of the typical features of many British films is their use of **social realism**. Social realism is a style of film-making which focuses on social and racial injustice and economic hardship by showing, as truthfully as possible, the struggles that many people have to endure. One of the ways in which this is done is to try to avoid stereotypes by showing characters that are complex, that are affected by the way that society is organised and that are neither absolutely good or bad. Many social realist films resist the temptation to complete each story with a neat **resolution**: this mirrors real life and also allows the audience to continue to engage, to think about the problems and injustices represented, after the film has finished.

Although *The Boy in the Striped Pyjamas* isn't a social realist film, it does contain elements of social realism. Think carefully about the representation of father: note down on your table the positive things about him which are particularly evident at the beginning of the film. Is patriotism and obedience to authority always seen as a bad thing in our society?

Bruno and Shmuel

Because the story is told through Bruno's eyes the camera often places us alongside him, at his level. This means we see what he sees and although we know things that he does not, this technique is effective, especially during the closing sequence. Bruno is always smartly dressed in well-fitting shorts, white shirt and sleeveless V-necked sweater, and he wears a suit at the party during the opening sequence. He is represented as a serious, thoughtful child who is treated in a fairly formal way,

Close up: the classroom

Character	Appearance	Techniques
BRUNO		
SHMUEL		
FATHER		
MOTHER		
GRETEL		
GRANDFATHER		
GRANDMOTHER		
PAVEL		
LIEUTENANT KOTLER		

- Copy the table above onto a piece of A4 paper. As you watch the whole film, or sequences from it, note down your general impressions of each character. Do we sympathise with them? Do our feelings change towards them during the film? Are they simply good or bad characters, or is their representation more complicated?

- Note down the techniques used to convey information about each character. Consider particular camera shots and angles and the use of diegetic and non-diegetic sound.

especially by his father. His costume reflects this. In contrast Shmuel's 'pyjamas' are too large and ill-fitting, they cover him from head to toe, his head is shaved. We view him through the barbed wire fence as we might view an animal in a zoo. Both boys are serious; Shmuel responds to questions but seldom asks them.

> 'The boy was smaller than Bruno and was sitting on the ground with a forlorn expression. He wore the same striped pyjamas that all the other people on that side of the fence wore and a striped cap on his head. He wasn't wearing any shoes or socks and his feet were rather dirty. On his arm he wore an armband with a star on it.' (*The Boy in the Striped Pyjamas*, page 106)

4: Shmuel gazes at a world beyond the fence

Close up: the classroom

Look carefully at the still above showing Shmuel.

- Focus carefully on **mise-en-scène**. What does it tell you about Shmuel and his situation?

- Compare the passage in the book describing Bruno's first impression of Shmuel with the still above. Do you think the director has managed to convey this impression effectively? What has he missed out? Does the mise-en-scène add anything that is not mentioned in the book?

The Final Sequence

Until the final sequence of the film, we do not see the boys together as Shmuel's face is constantly viewed through the fence and conversations, football and chess games take place separated by the wire. Neither Bruno nor Shmuel understand the symbolic relevance of the barbed wire fence that separates them. Mise-en-scène consistently reminds us of something the two friends seem almost unaware of – that they are physically and culturally separated. Shmuel is a Jew and prisoner of the Nazis. Bruno is the German son of the prison camp Commandant. Though the two are separated physically by a barbed wire fence, their lives become inescapably intertwined. The imagined story of Bruno and Shmuel sheds light on the brutality, senselessness and devastating consequences of war from an unusual point of view. Together, their tragic journey helps recall the millions of innocent victims of the Holocaust. As an eyewitness, a camp guard, who came forward during trials after the War reported:

At last, after 32 minutes, they are all dead...The dead, having nowhere to fall, stand like pillars...Even in death, families may be seen standing pressed together, clutching hands. It is only with great difficulty that the bodies are separated in order to clear the place for the next load.

- quoted in Martin Gilbert, *The Final Journey: the Fate of the Jews in Nazi Europe* (New York, 1979) and accessible at www.ibiblio.org/yiddish/Places/Buczacz/bucz-p4.htm

Close up: the classroom

- Listen carefully to the use of music in the final sequence. How is it used to drive the action of this final sequence? Concentrate on the moments of silence. What effect do these create?

- Focus on the way in which editing is used in order to build up tension in the sequence. Firstly, think about the speed. Where does the editing speed up and what effect does this have on the audience? Where does it slow and what effect does that create?

- Now think carefully about **cross-cutting**: how is this used to create a feeling of growing panic and fear? How many different groups do we follow in this story? What effect does the cutting between each group – the different **spheres of action** – have on the audience?

- Read through the eyewitness account of a gassing in a Nazi death camp. How is **cinematography** used to recreate the horror of the gas chamber? Are there any shots that you feel are particularly powerful? Describe the shot and how it makes you feel.

Key terms

Cross-cutting: Cutting between different sets of action that can be happening at the same time or at different times.

Spheres of action: The place, range or extent of what is happening at particular points in a story.

Cinematography: Camera shots, camera framing, camera movement and lighting. When making films, lighting is the responsibility of the 'cinematographer' – the Director of Photography. When studying film, lighting is frequently considered to be part of mise-en-scène, as in this book.

In this final sequence, both the audience and Bruno finally get to see life on the other side of the fence; until this point the reality of the camp has been kept out of sight. Bruno's knowledge of the camp, like many others at that moment in time, was based on what he had been told and seen in the propaganda films. The secret that Himmler said should 'never be spoken in public' is finally revealed. Director Mark Herman, however, does not create shock through the use of graphic images. We do not see the bodies; our last glimpse of the boys shows them clasping hands as the credits roll. The repeated close-up shot of the heavy iron door which leads to the gas chamber slowly zooms out to reveal the empty changing room with striped 'pyjamas' hanging from the coat hooks. And yet the ending is both shocking and moving. Editing, sound and cinematography work together to create a growing sense of panic and desperation which builds to a disturbing climax. Throughout the film we have typically viewed the world through Bruno's eyes. In the final sequence we view the growing panic of different groups. Editing enables us to follow individual characters, or sets of characters, as their desperation grows. Firstly, Maria as she discovers that Bruno is lost, then mother, then the boys exploring the camp looking for Shmuel's father. An eye-level tracking shot places us alongside the boys as they continue their search. We see Gretel, Maria and mother extend their search. We witness Bruno's first glimpse of the overcrowded hut and then cut to father and his soldiers as they join the hunt. This cross-cutting, which speeds up as the panic grows, allows us to witness the effect of the build up to the final tragedy on each of the central characters – this is no longer just Bruno's story.

Sound also creates a sense of desperation: a storm builds, becoming increasingly violent as father, Gretel and mother reach the place beside the fence where Bruno's clothes have been left. We may not see the corpses of the victims but the high-angle shot looking down at the naked bodies of the prisoners as they cling together in the chamber and the chilling low-angle shot of the porthole in the roof where the faceless, nameless soldier pours chemicals down onto the victims, is both chilling and memorable. The film has been evenly paced throughout, but by the end it is moving at a breathless pace. The story has moved from fable to history.

Industry and Creative Response

It is quite unusual for a family film to be about the Holocaust and perhaps it is not surprising that the film has caused a fair amount of critical debate. The Italian film *Life is Beautiful*, made in 1999, also caused a lot of controversy. In both cases the controversy revolved around the genre of the film – is it acceptable for the Holocaust to feature in films that can be seen by 12 year olds and are marketed as 'life affirming', 'inspirational' or 'inspiring'?

Although *The Boy in the Striped Pyjamas* is often referred to as a typically British film, it was produced by Miramax, which is owned by Disney. And it certainly feels like a 'typical' British film. It isn't 'glossy' and the emphasis is consistently on realism. The historical and social contexts were carefully researched and the story was told simply with events unfolding in chronological order. Lighting was designed to extend the feeling of realism and it tries hard to show the Holocaust through the eyes of a young German boy.

Marketing

Film Posters

The film poster for *The Boy in the Striped Pyjamas* was an important selling tool used by the film's distributors and exhibitors. All film posters are persuasive texts. They are designed to give audiences an introduction to the film and to encourage them to go and see it at the cinema.

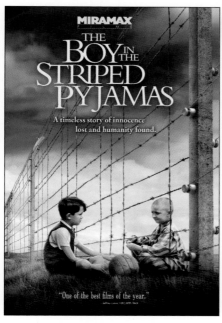

5: *The Boy...* poster

Close up: the classroom

- What do you notice first? Why do you think your eye is drawn to this?

- How does the text on the poster link to the images?

- What can you establish about this film just by looking at the poster?

- Why do you think this image has been chosen in order to 'sell' the film?

Close up: creative work

John Boyne, the author of *The Boy in the Striped Pyjamas* said that the film was *'made with honesty, passion and conviction by people who have great respect and admiration for those who survived, and great respect and admiration for those who did not. I do think it is very important to keep this story alive so we don't repeat it and anything we do to this end, any step we take to make one person look at the world a little bit differently I think is worth taking.'*

- Write a short review of the film considering how successful the film-makers were in achieving their aims.

Case Study 2
Rabbit-Proof Fence

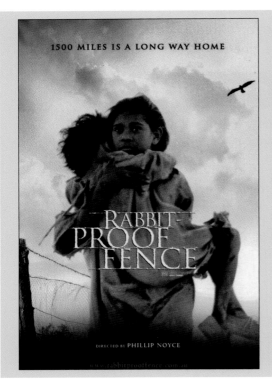

Country: Australia

Production Year: 2002

Director: Phillip Noyce

Certificate: PG

Main Awards:

Australian Film Institute 2002: Best Film, Best Sound, Best Original Musical Score, Best Cinematography

Denver International Film Festival: Best Feature-Length Film, People's Choice Award

In this section we will:

- Find out about the time and place in which the film is set.
- Focus upon the key themes and issues in *Rabbit-Proof Fence*.
- Explore the ways in which the 'micro' and 'macro' elements of film language are used to communicate ideas.

Synopsis

This is the true story of Molly Craig, a young black Australian girl who leads her younger sister and cousin in an escape from a government camp, set up as part of an official government policy to train them as domestic workers and integrate them into white society. With grit and determination Molly guides the girls on an epic journey, one step ahead of the authorities, over 1,500 miles of Australia's outback in search of the rabbit-proof fence that bisects the continent and will lead them home. These three girls are part of what is referred to today as the 'Stolen Generations'.

Close up: the classroom

In pairs, find a definition for the following terms:

- Aboriginal.
- Half-caste.
- Racism.

Introduction

The film *Rabbit-Proof Fence* is based on a book called *Follow the Rabbit-Proof Fence*, written by Doris Pilkington Garimara. This true story is based on the childhood memories of Doris's mother, who is its central character, Molly.

The action takes place in Australia in 1931 and highlights the despair experienced by Aboriginal mothers who had children by white fathers. These mothers had their children taken away from them in response to a government policy aimed at 'civilising' these young people and 'breeding out' their 'blackness'.

From the earliest years of European settlement in Australia, there is evidence of Aboriginal children being taken from their families as the authorities believed it was 'for their own good'. During the first half of the 20th century, it was official policy in most states to remove so-called half- or quarter-caste Aboriginal children.

Shockingly, this practice continued until the mid-1970s, and was only fully brought to public attention after the *Bringing Them Home* report was published in 1997. This report caused a lot of public discussion about what became known as the 'Stolen Generations'. Some people argued that the children were not 'stolen' but removed in order to give them a better life. Others were shocked by this practice, arguing it bore a frightening resemblance to Hitler's intention of creating a 'pure' Aryan race in Germany (a policy which ultimately led to the Holocaust).

However, there can be little doubt that thousands of Aboriginal children were taken from their families by force, or that their parents were 'tricked' into giving them up. The policy was definitely aimed at 'breeding out' Aboriginality, because only the so-called half- and quarter-caste children were taken. Fully Aboriginal half-brothers or sisters in the same families were left with their parents, while their 'lighter' children were removed. So, if the policy really aimed to offer Aboriginal children a better life, surely all children of allegedly 'bad mothers' would have been taken? In practice, the majority of the children removed went to missions, orphanages or children's homes where they were poorly

Key terms

Colonisation: Where a country takes over another country or territory and imposes its own laws and social structures, generally exploiting the economic resources of the colony. Britain colonised Australia, New Zealand, India and several territories in Africa for example. Other examples of colonisers were the French and Spanish.

Indigenous: People native to a country prior to its colonisation.

treated, struggled to find a sense of identity and experienced emotional or psychological problems.

Colonisation and the imposition of these sorts of policies played a big part in creating an **indigenous** 'underclass'. The Aboriginal people today make up the poorest group in Australia. Many were 'stolen' children, who continue to suffer the effects of the destruction of their identity, family life and culture.

The 'real' A. O. Neville

In 1905, Western Australia became the first state to pass an Aborigines Act which made the Chief Protector the legal guardian of 'every Aboriginal and part Aboriginal child' under sixteen years in the state.

From 1915 until 1936, Mr A. O. Neville was Chief Protector. He believed very strongly in the removal of 'part Aboriginal children' as a means of benefiting the whole community: 'the chief hope … of doing our human duty by the outcast is to take the children young and bring them up in a way that will establish their self-respect, make them useful units in the community and fit to live in it, according to its standards.' (A. O. Neville, 1938)

In 1931, the *Western Australian Aborigines Act* allowed for Neville to issue the order for the removal of the three girls, Molly, Gracie and Daisy, from their homes and families at Jigalong and be taken to the Moore River Settlement.

Themes and Issues

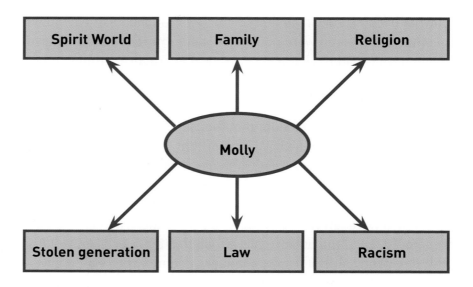

Law and Racism

Phillip Noyce, the film's director, carefully avoids a Hollywood 'good versus evil' dramatisation of Australia's colonial history. The representation of A. O. Neville shows us an unbending character who implements laws which we would view as racist today. However, it is important to understand that society was very different in the 1930s and the belief that Great Britain had a duty to 'civilise' the indigenous people of colonised countries was widely held. Although Neville ordered the removal of thousands of 'half-castes', he is portrayed as a man who genuinely believed in the moral and civilising benefits of his mission, and the superiority of white over native culture.

Presenting him in such a fashion rather than in embellished evil terms may evoke, from a British audience, a sense of guilt about the past – we are constantly told that Britain is 'Great', but here we see the actions of our country from a different perspective. We perhaps are made aware that life and people cannot easily be divided into simple categories such as good or evil, and that it is possible for people to do 'bad' things for what they believe are the 'right reasons'.

Overall, *Rabbit-Proof Fence* steers clear of preaching about the past. Its 'messages' are far more subtle: for example, we know that the Aboriginal servant who shelters Molly, Daisy and Grace, has been abused by her 'boss' but we do not see the abuse, it is only hinted at. Phillip Noyce avoids presenting the audience with painful images of oppression, violence and subjugation, instead opting for resoluteness, optimism, survival and hope. The central character, Molly, is clearly one of the many Aboriginals who have suffered from 'institutional racism' and yet she refuses to become a victim. She has spirit, she is the leader of the three girls, the one who holds on to her 'home' culture the most, who sees the Moore River settlement as 'sick', and decides to return home against all odds.

Religion: The Spirit World

Although the film is not overtly religious, religion and spirituality are present in many forms at several levels, and are vital components of the film. The film shows two very different cultures and their religious practices form an important element in the way the story is told. When we first encounter Neville he is given the opportunity through dialogue to demonstrate that he truly believes he is right, as he explains his position to the white, Christian women in the lecture theatre. He appears to care about his legal charges (the Aboriginal children), and has a detailed knowledge of each one – who had new shoes, and when – despite the size of territory under his authority.

However, our sympathies are directed not only towards the girls, but also towards the culture that they represent. We see the world through the girls' eyes and Neville and the culture he represents is therefore seen as dominating and alien.

For example, our initial introduction to Neville is a low-angle shot to his face from the level of his desk. He is lit up against the projector screen; the rest of the room is in darkness. Lighting and camera framing combine to create the impression of a powerful, threatening character and the metal 'pointer' he holds in his hand adds to this impression. The beginning of his lecture bridges the terrible moments of agony we witness when Molly's mother and grandmother throw themselves into the dust after the girls have been captured.

Throughout the film Neville is always superior to the camera position. This is clearly shown in the scene at the Moore River settlement when Molly is inspected by Neville. In this sequence the camera takes the subjective position of the girl, and we look up at Neville who is bending forwards and filling the visual field. The soundtrack distorts and distances his voice. Throughout the sequence, we are positioned with Molly not only physically, but also emotionally. It is not only Neville who is distanced, but also the Moore River Settlement itself. It is always viewed from the far end of the compound, using a low camera angle in which the church is positioned centrally and appears to be on the top of an incline.

6: For thine is the kingdom, the power and the glory, for ever and ever?

Close up: the classroom

Study the mise-en-scène in the frame above. Look carefully at the framing of A.O.Neville and note down the effect this may have on the audience.

- What do his costume, facial expression, hairstyle and notebook suggest to you about this character?

- If you had to guess what he did for a living, what might he do? Which other elements of the mise-en-scène inform your guess?

Cinematography and sound consistently work together throughout the film in order to call into question the 'God given' right of the white settlers to impose their values and beliefs upon the Aboriginal people. The Aboriginals love and respect their environment, they acknowledge its power and beauty, their spiritual beliefs and values are shown as strong and positive and stand in stark contrast to those of the white settlers.

Close up: the classroom

Key Sequence 1

Review the opening sequence. What do we learn about the spirit bird in this sequence?

- Which other elements of film language suggest that the spirit world is important in Aboriginal culture?
- When does the spirit bird reappear in the narrative? What is its role?

Key Sequence 2

Review the sequence (approx 1.11.30 – 1.13.45) where Molly and Daisy fall down in the desert and are called home by their mother and the spirit bird.

- How is emotional tension created in this scene through editing and camera angles?
- What is the effect of the music on your emotions? Can you explain why it has this effect?

Key Sequence 3

Review the final sequence – the meeting (1.17.50 – 1.23.00).

- Why is the spirit bird used at the beginning of this sequence?
- Why has the director used slow motion for the meeting?
- What is the effect of seeing Molly and Daisy with their mother and grandmother at their camp?
- What is your reaction to seeing footage of the real Molly and Daisy at the end of the film? Why do you think the director included this footage?

The spirit bird plays an important role in the film – it conveys a universal theme. It demonstrates the power of nature and the ability of human beings to overcome the most terrible obstacles. Throughout history so many people have been dominated and forced to give up what was sacred to them. We often focus on the struggles of one person, or small group, when we think about how oppression can be overcome. For example, the struggles of all the black people in South Africa and America were symbolised through the imprisonment of Nelson Mandela and the speeches of Martin Luther King. Molly's continued struggle, the fact that she was sent back again and again to Moore River, also symbolises the continued struggle of the Aboriginal people in Australia.

Genre and Style

Rabbit-Proof Fence is a true story, based on the memories of Doris Pilkington's mother. After reading the book, screenwriter Christine Olsen was so moved by the story that she decided to adapt it for the screen. She was very clear about the kind of director she wanted to help make the film because it was important that the style was appropriate. This was not a Hollywood film; careful research was necessary in order to maintain the integrity of the story. *Rabbit-Proof Fence* is based on a particular period in history but it also carries a message about our world today and the need to respect other people's cultures. In many ways the film employs a social realist style and imperative (see *The Boy in the Striped Pyjamas*).

The film 'feels' distinctly Australian in its use of the land as **iconic**, but it also has, at its heart, a universal narrative structure – the journey. Journeying is one of the most common themes in literature and film. This journey usually involves a personal search; characters are trying to find their place in the world and the journey involves growth, finding inner strength, discovering a 'spirit' that will not be extinguished by outside forces, no matter how powerful (see 'Religion: The Spirit World' section for the significance of the spirit bird).

The journey in *Rabbit-Proof Fence* begins when the girls escape from the Moore River settlement to which they are sent. Ironically, their 'guide' home is the rabbit-proof fence built by white settlers to stop rabbits spreading myxomatosis from one half of Australia to the other. The fence is highly **symbolic**, erected to contain the spread of disease – the laws enforced by Neville could also be viewed as an attempt to contain the disease of 'blackness' that threatened white Australian society. The journey involves a long, hard trek for Molly, Grace and Daisy, across 1200 miles of desert and bush. It is Molly's spirit that inspires the return home to their land and their mothers.

The film is told in a steady, unsentimental tone that allows the film to be powerful without the typical Hollywood use of sweeping music. It is the simplicity and truth of the story that creates the emotion. Most of the Aboriginal roles were played by non-professional actors, again bringing a sense of realism to the characters. The performances of the children, untrained in acting, have an honesty, simplicity and dignity, with most of the girls' inner feelings conveyed through facial expression. At the end of the film we see real footage of the ageing Molly, again conveying a sense of realism and overall suggesting hope tinged with sadness.

Christopher Doyle (cinematographer) creates a beautiful vision of the Australian Outback. The importance of cinematography is established in the opening sequence: time is taken to show the barren beauty of Western Australia which is revealed initially in a series of aerial shots and then in mid- and long shots showing the light sparkling through the leaves of the trees and huge clear blue sky overhead.

The sound is also superb. The diegetic sounds of the natural world – rhythmic footsteps, birds screeching, the crunching and banging of the landscape – combine with non-diegetic sound to create a sense of the spirit world. We do not get a tourist board view of Australia. This setting has a life and spirit all of its own and plays an important part in the story.

Close up: the classroom

Now rewatch the opening sequence with commentary from the director (Phillip Noyce) and screenwriter (Christine Olsen).

- What kind of place is Jigalong?

- How is Christine treated by its 300 Aboriginal residents?

- What do you learn about their way of life today? What kinds of things are important? Has much changed since the 1930s when Molly was a child?

- How is cinematography used to convey the remote nature of the setting?

The music, an adaptation of Aboriginal melodies by Peter Gabriel, is haunting and effective. The camerawork never allows the beauty of the Australian outback to eclipse the human element – an impressive feat when considering how glorious the countryside is. Christopher Doyle, the cinematographer, takes us on a journey through the vast Australian landscape, the barren deserts and lonely outposts in the relentless heat of the day, the multi-coloured skies and the hidden shadows of the night. The look is bleached and untouched.

Rabbit-Proof Fence has little dialogue and relies greatly on images, sounds and rhythms to tell the story. Noyce's direction, Doyle's cinematography and Gabriel's music give a spiritual feeling to moments of emotional intensity, such as the tearing of children from their mothers, the seemingly endless journey across a daunting barren landscape and the homecoming embrace between Molly and her mother.

Representation, genre and narrative structure

7: Molly leads the way back home

Molly is clearly the film's 'hero'. She leads her sister and cousin back to their home and family. She encounters many obstacles on her journey, problems she must solve such as lack of food and water, keeping Daisy and Gracie safe and how to avoid the police and the Aboriginal tracker, Moodo. She has to stay focused in spite of the hardships and dangers. She is only a child herself but she must survive in an adult world and show the ability to outwit her pursuers. The 1500 mile journey is not simply a journey home, it is a '**rite of passage**' during which Molly learns much about herself and the outside world. It is a rejection of the white man's law. Molly may be young but she underlines the importance of family and the need to respect and understand people's cultural roots.

Molly's role as hero is established in the opening sequence of the film and her heroic qualities develop as the narrative progresses.

Opening credit sequence of *Rabbit-Proof Fence*

There are two equally important elements in this sequence: the setting and Molly, the central character. We hear Aboriginal voices chanting over the credits, which conveys a feeling of 'otherness'. We are about to enter an unfamiliar, mystical world, where nature is viewed as a sacred, powerful force. The aerial shot which opens the film travels over and looks down upon the vast, dry landscape of Western Australia. We see no houses or roads, simply mile after mile of bush land. Eventually, the camera tilts down to reveal a dirt track and a few small buildings, then cuts to a mid-shot of Molly. She is not shown as separate from her environment but appears to be just one element of the natural world, framed by the trees and sky, her eyes shining as she smiles and watches an eagle circling above her. Later her mother tells her the eagle is a 'spirit bird' which will protect her wherever she goes.

8: Molly watches the 'spirit bird' and leads the search for the Iguana

When we first see Molly with her sister Daisy and cousin Gracie she is leading the group. She is bigger and looks physically stronger than the other two girls. She can already follow the tracks of the iguana and spot it when it lies camouflaged between the branches of the tree. Already it is obvious that she has skills not yet learnt by the other girls; her mother and grandmother are proud of her – she must not be taken away: 'Tell Mr. A. O. Neville he's not having my Molly.'

Close up: the classroom

Review the opening sequence (00.05 – 05.45).

- What establishes Molly as the central character?

- How do the 'micro' elements of film language convey the fact that Molly is happy in Jigalong?

- What sort of person is she? List her heroic qualities and describe how these are represented.

- Who narrates in this sequence? Is it the young or old Molly? What effect does this have?

The opening sequence has shown us the things that are important in Molly's life: her family, her culture, her environment. Her resistance shows us how she feels about being taken away and her strength of spirit. If we play on and pause on the final image of this sequence we see mother and grandmother lying in the dust on the ground. Grandmother's despair is underlined by the terrible way in which she beats herself over the head; the external pain cannot make the emotional pain of losing her grand-daughter go away. It is at this moment and over this image that we are introduced to another key character, Mr. A. O. Neville. We hear him before we see him.

Mr. A. O. Neville

During the opening credits, even before we have seen the images of the Australian outback, we are given some information onscreen about The Western Australian Aboriginies Act and the man responsible for enforcing it, A.O. Neville:

- For 100 years, the Aboriginal peoples have resisted the invasion of their land by white settlers.

- Now, a special law, The Western Australian Aborigines Act (1931), controls their lives in every detail.

- Mr A. O. Neville, the Chief Protector of Aborigines, is the legal guardian of every Aborigine in the state of Western Australia.

- He has the power ' to remove any half-caste child' from their family anywhere within the State.

9: A lecture on colonialism

Close up: the classroom

Watch the sequence which introduces A. O. Neville (approximately 011.10 – 13.25).

- Why has Phillip Noyce, the director, chosen to put a sound bridge in at this point?

- What is your first impression of Neville? What effect does lighting and camera shots have on that impression?

- What do we learn about Neville's view of the Aboriginals in this sequence?

Close up: the classroom

- Look carefully at the stills below from a slightly later sequence (starting at approximately 20 minutes into the film). Consider carefully all the elements of mise-en-scène. Write a short explanation of what is communicated to the audience about characters and setting through the mise-en- scène.

10: Breeding out the blackness

Although we do not see Neville in the opening ten minutes of the film, his influence in the lives of the people who live in the tiny community of Jigalong is already clearly evident. Riggs the policeman talks about him as he watches from his horse as Molly and her friends play. Molly's mother tells the storekeeper who has control of the rations to tell Neville he cannot take Molly. There is a sense conveyed that no one can escape his power and influence; his word is law, everything in the state comes under his control. Throughout the film he is repeatedly shown in low-angle shots which slightly distort his image and give the feeling that he is constantly looking down on those he should be protecting rather than controlling. Actor Kenneth Branagh presents us with a picture of a stiff, unbending character. His hair is slicked down and does not move; even in the hottest weather he wears a thick suit, shirt and tie. He rarely smiles; he controls his own emotions with the same rigidity that he controls the lives of others. He is a cold, unemotional character who is not apparently moved by the obvious pain that he inflicts upon the families that he breaks up. However, there is more to Neville than the stereotypical 'baddie'. We may have little sympathy for him but he is shown as someone who wants to 'improve' the lives of the Aboriginals, no matter how misguided his methods. Neville represents a particular way of thinking at a particular moment in world history. The British Empire was built on ideas of 'civilizing' other countries and cultures in the certain knowledge that Britain knew what was best for them. Tragically this process of colonising other countries often led to the suffering of the **indigenous** people and the destruction of their way of life.

Moodoo

Phillip Noyce does not overlook the irony of the past, in particular the assimilation of Aboriginals into white culture. This is most clearly illustrated by the 'tracker', who enforces 'law' and captures any kids who escape from the settlement. He seems to accept that his daughter has to be removed from his family 'for her own good'. However, in very subtle ways he demonstrates a glimmer of admiration at the ability of the three girls to escape so successfully. He does as he is told by his 'masters' but manages to show that there is more to his personality; he can undermine in subtle, non-confrontational ways. He can work with the system whilst refusing to accept its values and maintaining his own sense of identity. Interestingly, the 'tracker' is played by David Gupilil, who starred as a boy in a groundbreaking film, *Walkabout* (Nicolas Roeg, 1971), which explored conflict between white and aboriginal people in Australia at that time.

Close up: the classroom

In groups, brainstorm Moodoo's character by concentrating on his role at Moore River, and then his role in the recovery of the girls. Discuss the following questions and include specific examples from the film:

- How is he presented to the audience (positively, negatively, sympathetically, or as a villain)?

- What does he do and say, and what do facial expressions tell us about the sort of person he is?

- What is revealed about Moodoo's character in the scenes where he returns a runaway girl to the Moore River Settlement and where Neville talks to him about his request to return to his tribal home?

- Does he really want to catch the girls? How do we know?

Industry – Selling the Film

Although this is a specifically Australian story – one which centres on the Stolen Generations and the White Australia Policy – it is told in a way that emphasises universal elements of tragedy and heroism. This allows a broader, more widespread audience appeal. To maximise this appeal, *Rabbit-Proof Fence*'s release was accompanied by a considerable marketing campaign including a mini-documentary focusing on the casting search for three Aboriginal girls which took place across Australia.

The director, Phillip Noyce, personally premiered the film at various locations throughout Australia. He gave numerous interviews, a study guide was produced and the book on which the film was based was republished, featuring images from the film on its cover.

This marketing strategy was partly based on an assumption that Australian audiences may have been reluctant to see a film about indigenous Australians and colonial history. So, the focus was moved onto other areas that were more likely to 'sell' the film to a wider audience: the 'melodrama' of casting the three young leads, recounting stories of what it was like to work with non-professional actors, the emotion on set during the filming of the scene where a white police officer forcibly removes the three children from their mother's arms . Even turning the young actresses into celebrities, who appeared on magazine covers, telling their individual stories to magazine audiences, was a way of marketing the film without focusing on the less marketable, controversial issues of the film.

The trailer

Another important way of 'selling' a film to an audience is the trailer, where key moments are put together with titles and music in order to persuade audiences to watch the film.

Close up: the classroom

Watch the trailer on imdb.com

- What can you say about the style or look of the film, based on the trailer? You could look at characters' appearance and costume design as well as the time and place in which the film is set.

- What do you think is the narrative or story of the film? In what different ways does the trailer reveal this to us?

- What kinds of people do you think might want to go and see this film? How is the trailer designed to persuade people to watch it?

DVD Release

The DVD cover for a film is also a persuasive text, designed to convey a wide range of messages to different audiences. It should encourage people to pick up the film if they see it in a shop; it should clearly identify the film; it should make anyone who sees it want to watch the film. The cover uses images, language and logos to convey messages.

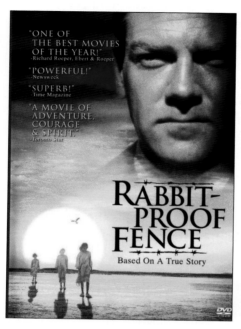

11: *Rabbit Proof-Fence* DVD cover

Close up: the classroom

Look closely at the DVD cover for *Rabbit-Proof Fence* and record your first impressions in three sentences. Now look closely at the following aspects of the cover, in each case thinking about the purpose, the intended audience and the overall impact of each element:

- Images chosen: which of the characters are featured?

- Why is Kenneth Branagh (A. O. Neville) given prominence?

- What ideas are conveyed by the design of the cover? Think carefully about colour and the ways in which characters and objects are incorporated into the design.

- Text: what information or ideas are conveyed? What different styles of writing are used?

- Graphics (e.g. logos)

- Layout devices (such as text boxes)

Part 4 Controlled Assessment

In this section we will:

- Outline the different controlled assessment options.
- Provide ideas to get you started.
- Give tips on how to get the best mark for each of the options.

Introduction

The controlled assessment pulls together learning from every aspect of the course and should emphasise what you know about film language, the film industry and film production. The controlled assessment is made up of 2 sections and you are required to produce 6 items.

Film Exploration	Industry research (350–500 words)	Investigating the **production**, **distribution** and **exhibition** of a film of your choice.
	Analysis of a short extract (350–750 words)	Written analysis of a short extract from the same film, exploring how **2 micro** aspects of film language are used to create meaning.
Film Production	Pitch (150 words)	A 'sales pitch' and logline for a new film.
	Pre-production	Using the same film idea as the one you have pitched you must produce **one** of the following: a **screenplay**, a **storyboard**, a **magazine cover and contents page** or a **marketing campaign**.
	Production	This should also be based on the pitch.* You must produce **one** of the following: a **short film sequence**, a **website**, a **magazine feature**, a **poster campaign** or a **press pack**.
	Evaluative Analysis	An analysis of your final production which also demonstrates your understanding of film language, organisations and audiences.

*If you work as a group to produce the short film sequence then only one person's pitch needs to be used. You need to make this clear in the evaluative analysis of your work.

Film Exploration

Task 1 – Industry Research

Looking into a film's 'organisational' context – the things surrounding its **production**, **distribution** and **exhibition** – can reveal many things about the film industry and the research component of the controlled assessment is designed to do this by focusing on the three broad areas of the industry.

This task requires you to undertake research into a film of your choice, select relevant information and draw conclusions on what this information tells us about this film and the way that the film industry operates.

Production

This relates to the making of the film from its point of conception, which may be a pitch or a screenplay (more on these later) or even a suggestion from a star's agent about what kind of film the star they represent may want to appear in next. You should investigate the source material for the film, the production company, the financial context and people involved in the production. The following questions may give you a place to start:

Key research questions – production

Which production company made the film?

- Where is it based?
- What else is it known for?

Source material

- Where did the idea for the film come from?
- What genre is the film?

Who was involved in the production?

- What is the producer/executive producer known for?
- Have they made any similar films?
- Do they have a successful track record?
- Who wrote the screenplay?
- Which stars are involved?

The film's financing

- How much was the budget?
- Did it go over budget? If so, why?

Production background

- Where was it filmed?
- Can you find information on any interesting events during the production?

Distribution

There are two distinct aspects to film distribution: the physical distribution of the film's 'prints' (by 2013, in digital form) which must be duplicated and delivered to the cinema and the film's marketing. As well as some background on the film's distribution you are required to include a minimum of **three examples of how the film was marketed and/or promoted**. This is good preparation for some of the creative controlled assessment tasks.

Key research questions – distribution

Distribution company/companies

- Who was the distributor in the UK/US?

Prints/Digital copies

- Did the film have a global release or was it released country by country?
- Can you find out how many prints/digital copies of the film were released in the US and the UK?

Marketing and Promotion

- What was the film's marketing budget?
- How was the film marketed? (3 examples)
- Do you know anything about the film's promotion?

Exhibition

This refers to where and how the film is shown – most obviously at the cinema and at home on DVD, television or (increasingly) the web. This is the area we are most familiar with, but it can reveal many things if you spend some time investigating what went on when the film was on general release.

Key terms

Marketing & Promotion: All the different ways a film is 'publicised'. The key distinction is that marketing is advertising created by the distributor and costs money and promotion is how other media – like TV programmes or magazines – publicise a film through interviews and features, for example, and costs the distributor nothing.

Key research questions – exhibition

Cinema

- What types of cinema was the film shown in?
- Were there any special versions (3D or IMAX)?
- How long was it on for?

Success

- How much did it make at the box office?
- Can you find out how much it made through DVD sales?

The research will probably take a while and you should use a range of sources and cross reference these, as some of the information you find may be contradictory. There is a range of websites where you can find information on these things but the following are particularly useful:

IMDb - www.imdb.com

The Internet Movie Database has information on all three of the areas above and may be a good starting point.

Wikipedia – www.wikipedia.com

This can be great for finding out background information such as who was originally going to play the main character or why the director walked out halfway through filming. Remember: anybody can edit a 'wiki' entry. Try to cross-reference your findings.

Box Office Mojo – www.boxofficemojo.com

This is possibly the most reliable site looking into film distribution, and you can search for individual films. This is a site based in the US so you may need to cross-reference some of your findings.

Close up: creative work

- Don't just copy and paste the information: engage with your findings – what do they tell you about this film/the film industry?
- Only include information that is interesting. If you are going to include the box-office takings for Portugal, you need to explain why and if you don't know then don't include it!

Below is a real example of research carried out by one GCSE student on the film *V for Vendetta*. Jack Farmer begins his findings with the title and release date of the film.

Film: *V for Vendetta*	Year: 2005

After his title he selects interesting points from the research that he has carried out on the way in which the film was **produced**. All films begin with an idea and in this case the idea came from a comic book. Other important findings are also touched on, for example, who directed and produced the film, how it was financed and which actors were involved.

Production Details

The idea came from Alan Moore a.k.a The Wizard of Northampton and was first published in the 1980s as a black-and-white comic book, 'Warrior'. The Wachowski brothers produced the film and wrote the screenplay and James McTeigue directed (famous for his first assistant director position in all of the *Matrix* films). It was made by Virtual Studios and Silver Pictures. This American film was partly financed by Medienboard Berlin-Brandenburg GMBH. The film had a budget of 67 million dollars and featured a high profile cast of actors including American star Natalie Portman and many British and Irish actors like Stephen Fry, Stephen Rea and John Hurt.

In the **distribution** section Jack carefully selected interesting points that he felt were important in terms of industry needs. He shows that Warner Bros. has different companies in different countries. His facts underline the way in which the release of films is often tied in with the big film festivals and the need to reach an international market. He talks about certain strategies used within the marketing campaign and shows how carefully distributors and producers plan their release dates.

Distribution details

Warner Bros. Pictures Distribution was the USA distributor. The UK distributor was Warner Bros. Pictures International. It was test screened at the Berlin film festival where it was a hit and first shown in its home country, America, before being released globally. The film was very successful in marketing because it featured a popular topic. The success of *The Matrix* and *The Matrix* Trilogy (also created by the Wachowski Bros.) was also used to sell the film. It also related to current issues about threats of terrorism in London. The marketing campaign included masks of 'V', teaser posters and trailers that

---

were full of mystery and action leaving unanswered questions about what was to happen on the 5th November. The global dimension of the film was reflected in its marketing materials, for example, the poster featured 'People should not be afraid of their governments but governments should be afraid of their people'. Unfortunately the terrorist attacks of 7/7 in 2005 coincided with the UK release of *V for Vendetta*, and the release was then postponed due to the sensitivity of the subject at that point in time.

Jack's **exhibition** details, although brief, cover several of the important areas involved in the screening of films. He points out the types of cinema that screened *V for Vendetta* and could have linked this information with the target audiences mentioned in his Production and Distribution sections. He underlines the importance of choosing a release date in terms of attracting the widest possible audience, and the need to be aware of subject matter when it could reflect current sensitive issues. He considers ratings in both Britain and the USA , box-office receipts, fan bases and different media ' platforms' that follow the cinema release (Video, DVD and Blu-ray).

Exhibition details

It was shown in all types of cinemas (multiplex/independent/arthouse), again reflecting the expectation of a very wide audience. It was due for release on the 5th November (Guy Fawkes Night) in order to create maximum impact in terms of its narrative. This date was postponed (see above) but it was in release for a total of 105 days/15 weeks. The worldwide lifetime grosses were $132,511,035 with 36% of that from the first weekend; $1.4 million just came from IMAX cinema revenue. The film had a British rating of 15 and an American rating of R. The screenplay has a comic book history but the film was more of an action genre, so the target audience was very wide as you have traditional comic book fans and families who enjoy thrillers. It is available on video/DVD and Blu-ray.

Close up: the classroom

- Can you think of any other areas of production, distribution and exhibition that could have been explored in this research?

It's worth noting that this research task is worth 10 marks, so your teacher will give you ample time to complete this task. The work you do in this unit is great preparation for your production unit and your two final exams, so it's important to make sure that you understand what is involved in production, distribution and exhibition – the three key areas of the film industry.

Task 2 – A 'Micro' Analysis of a Short Extract from the Same Film

Jack then went on to complete his analysis of the micro elements of film language on the film he had focused on in his research. You will have learnt a lot about the micro (and macro) elements of film language at the beginning of the course. This is your chance to show the knowledge and understanding you have gained and to communicate the ways in which a sequence from your favourite film 'talks' to an audience. Make sure you are clear about the ways in which each of the micro features work and can use the correct terminology. You must choose two areas to focus on from this list:

- Cinematography

- Editing

- Sound

- Mise-en-scène.

It's a good idea to go back to the Film Language section at the beginning of this book and remind yourself about the terminology used for each element of film language and the ways in which they are used to create meaning and audience response in certain films. Take time to pick the extract you want to analyse. Look for one that gives you lots to talk about and be prepared to watch it over and over again!

Jack begins with the title given in the specification and then uses the opening paragraph to put the extract into context and to give brief reasons for his choice. I have only included the first few paragraphs of Jack's work and have highlighted parts of the analysis that demonstrate his use of appropriate film terminology, his understanding of the ways in which film language creates meaning, and his consideration of the ways in which an audience might respond. Even reading only part of his analysis shows how confident he is in all three areas. When you complete your analysis make sure you include these areas and don't forget to include your own response – how it made you feel. After all, you are an extremely important member of your film's intended audience!

'Explore the ways in which two micro elements of film language create meanings and responses in one sequence from your chosen film.' *V FOR VENDETTA* (1:47:29 – 1:52:52): cinematography and mise-en-scène.

The sequence I have chosen is from my favourite film, *V for Vendetta*; it is meant to be full of tension in the build up to the revolution and shows a fight between 'V' and the officials. The director builds tension with film language; the sequence shows the build up to the death of 'V' and the revolution.

The sequence starts with a high-angled crane establishing shot looking at a part of London's city centre, present throughout the whole of the film, with an advertising screen attached to a building playing the Chancellor's speech. The diegetic sound of the Chancellor's voice booms out and is used as a sound bridge and non-diegetic fast music plays, building the tension for the audience as the screen cuts from the city centre to several close-ups and medium shots of televisions showing the same speech. At this moment in the scene the television rooms are packed with people but as the scene goes on the rooms empty showing how fewer people are listening to the Chancellor and more are joining the revolution.

A man enters the underground and he is obviously the most senior official as he is the only one wearing a suit and two men are at his side implying they are his personal bodyguards, and then a man refers to him as 'Sir'. We then briefly cut back to the television which ends after just one full sentence from the Chancellor, before we return to the subterranean hall where the senior official positioned in the middle of three other men now looks at his watch in urgency as another says 'Where is he?' The tension is now heightened as the audience all want to know when 'V' is going to show himself.

After a quick mid-shot of a television shot of the Chancellor's speech we go back to the senior official looking at his watch when 'V' speaks, saying 'Penny for the guy', referring to 'Where is he?' The camera cuts to a medium shot of 'V' in the middle of the screen with his mask illuminated by the shining torches of every official aiming straight at him from around the room. This makes 'V' the centre of attention and everyone's eyes in the film and the audience are glued to his face. While we once again cut back to the television now talking about an enemy/ terrorist wishing to divide the nation ,'V' is searched with a metal detector by a cautious official not taking his eyes off 'V' showing that this has been planned, referring back to 'Where is he?', but the officials are still wary.

We now cut back to the various television shots. But this time they are not close-ups of just the television but medium shots of the rooms with the televisions in. One of these rooms is a pub that earlier in the film is crowded and now is empty with no-one even behind the bar. This is done to show that no-one is actually there and the speech you have been listening to is falling on deaf ears. The rooms are still lit up though, producing a clever cliché. The lights are on but no-one's home. This is telling us that the public are joining the revolution.

Continues...

– Jack Farmer, 2010 (reprinted with permission)

When you read through Jack's work you can clearly see how good he is at accurately naming the types of shot and camera movement that are used. He doesn't just describe what is happening; he considers what effect is being created. He doesn't waste words – almost every sentence provides evidence of a good understanding.

Close up: creative work

- Re-watch your chosen sequence several times and make notes on the areas of film language that you have chosen to focus on.

- Pick an extract that is about 3 minutes long and gives you lots to talk about.

- Don't tell the examiner what happens in the rest of the film, just focus on your sequence.

- Make sure you have only looked at two micro elements of film language and that after you have described, for example, what kind of shot is used you talk about its effect on an audience.

- Take time to redraft your analysis. Listen carefully to your teacher's comments on your work and try to incorporate their suggestions for improving your response.

Film Production

The Pitch

'Pitching' refers to the process whereby film-makers present ideas for new films to producers and potential investors who may be interested in developing the idea. It is best thought of as a sales pitch, where the film's attractive features are summarised. This usually takes place in a meeting, where the film-makers may only have one minute to convince a producer that the idea is worth developing.

A good pitch should explain the film's narrative and the major plot points from the beginning to the end (no producer wants to invest in a film without being told that the main hero dies at the end).

You really need to think about the suitability of your idea and whether it would attract a producer to spend money on the film.

Key things a pitch should cover:

Logline	A one-sentence summary of the film to hook the producer.
Characters	The main character and any other significant characters.
Narrative	An overview of the beginning, middle and end of the film's narrative.
Genre	Refer to the film's genre as appropriate.
Possible Stars	Films that could attract or make use of established stars have the potential to make more money.
Similar Films	This can help potential producers get an idea of the kind of film and, more importantly, show that there is an established audience for this kind of film.

Logline

The key thing to producing a successful logline is to remember the audience. Loglines are not aimed at the film's audience; in fact the audience may never even know what a film's logline is. This should be made separate from a film's tagline, which is used to attract the audience by giving them a taste of what it is about. The comparison of the logline and taglines below should make the difference clear.

> **Key terms**
>
> **Plot points:** The major events that take place in a film which help to shape the film's narrative.

Avatar

Logline	A paraplegic marine is given the chance to walk again as he goes in search of Intel on the distant planet Pandora, but finds more than he was looking for.
Tagline	Enter the world.

Alien

Logline	A mining ship, investigating a suspected SOS lands on a distant planet. The crew discover strange creatures and soon their investigation becomes a battle for survival.
Tagline	In space, no one can hear you scream.

The logline should be used to make one or more of the following aspects of the film clear:

The Premise – the basic idea for the film, the story and the themes.

Character – at least the main character.

Genre – this should be clear if you have covered the previous points successfully.

Close up: the classroom

Rank the following three loglines for the same film in order of success (from good to bad). Discuss your reasons with a friend.

- A 'stag night' in Vegas goes badly wrong when the groom mysteriously disappears.

- A group of men go to Las Vegas with hilarious consequences.

- After a heavy night of drinking, 3 friends must retrace their steps to find the bridegroom before the wedding.

It is fine if the logline is very direct as long as it covers the elements listed above. The key thing is to make sure a potential producer understands the type of film you are trying to get made. If it's not clear to them then it may not be clear to an audience and they won't invest.

Having hooked your potential producer with the logline, the pitch needs to give a more complete idea of your film in 150 words.

Close up: creative work

- Make sure the logline is clearly distinguishable from the pitch.

- Spend time developing your idea so that it can be easily conveyed – clear genres and easy to understand narratives work best here.

- The best pitches are a paragraph of continuous writing – bullet points do not show your understanding of the pitching process.

- It should be written in a way that could easily be read out.

- Don't waste your time including lots of additional information that is not required, such as filming locations or budget.

- Remember – the film hasn't been made so it doesn't star Shia LaBeouf and Eva Mendes, you are only suggesting the type of star who would be appropriate.

Pre-Production

Screenplay

A film script is referred to as a screenplay to distinguish it from other media forms. The screenplay is a key part of the planning process and is a blueprint for the film, and goes beyond what is said by the characters to include detail on all of the significant things that the audience would see or hear when watching the film.

The best preparation for this task is to read an existing screenplay. There are many websites which have screenplays which can be viewed for free. You might even try searching to see if the screenplay for a film you like is available.

Key ingredients of a screenplay

- Detailed description of mise-en-scène.

- Clear indications of the action that is taking place.

- Clear indications of what the audience would hear.

Over the past 80 or so years, the screenplay itself has developed a set of conventions which you should include:

Format   Most professional screenplays use **Courier** typeface in size **12**.

As well as giving the appearance of old scripts produced

on a typewriter, this also roughly equates to a minute per page, so the duration of the scenes/films can quickly be established.

Slug Line   An introduction to the scene. This indicates where the action will take place. A new slug line should be included every time there is a change of location. It begins with an indication of whether it is an interior (indoor) or exterior (outdoor) location (INT or EXT). There should then be a brief description of the location and finally an indication as to whether the scene takes place at day or at night. In most professional screenplays this is aligned to the left in upper case (capitals) separated by full stops.

Example:

```
INT. WAREHOUSE. DAY.
```

Scene Description   A description of everything that the audience would see and hear when watching the film. It should be written in the present tense (as though it is happening right now). It should be detailed enough to let the reader picture the film in their heads. Professional screenplays do not usually contain references to camerawork (angle, movement) unless it is particularly relevant to the way the story is being told. References to characters, sounds and, if needed, film language should be upper case.

Example:

The warehouse roller shutter begins to rise and a WARNING ALARM is heard. A black limousine pulls into the warehouse and pulls up at the side of a large steel crate. The door opens and TWO HEAVIES dressed in black suits get out of the car. They walk to the rear of the car and there is a HIGH ANGLE as the boot opens to reveal TOM BAXTER tied up and gagged. They pull TOM from the car and carry him to the steel crate which we now see is padlocked.

Character Heading   This indicates when a character is speaking. It should be upper case and indented to approximately the centre of the page.

Dialogue   What the characters say. You do not need to include
directions on how this should be spoken. Any reference
to what the character is doing whilst they speak should be
clear in the scene description that comes before and after.

Example:

```
                         HEAVY
              Now give us the code.
                          TOM
         I told you, I don't know the code.
          I'm just the delivery boy. They
                 never told me the code.
```

Putting it all together:

```
INT. WAREHOUSE. DAY.

The warehouse roller shutter begins to rise
and a WARNING ALARM is heard. A black
limousine pulls into the warehouse and pulls
up at the side of a large steel crate. The
door opens and TWO HEAVIES dressed in black
suits get out of the car. They walk to the
rear of the car and there is a HIGH ANGLE as
the boot opens to reveal TOM BAXTER tied up
and gagged. They pull TOM from the car and
carry him to the steel crate which we now see
is padlocked.
                         HEAVY
              Now give us the code.
                          TOM
         I told you, I don't know the code.
          I'm just the delivery boy. They
                 never told me the code.
The HEAVIES look at one another in a puzzled
way and one of them pulls a mobile phone from
inside his jacket.
```

Close up: creative work

- Let the visuals do the talking. Few professional screenplays have pages and pages of dialogue. Get a friend to tell you if they could picture the scene clearly in their minds.

- Dialogue can be very tricky to get right. It's a good idea to read it out aloud, and get a friend to tell you whether it sounds right.

Storyboard

The storyboard can be an essential part of the pre-production on any film as it allows the film-makers to see how shots will work together in a sequence. It also allows for changes to be made before the (far more expensive) shoot begins. Storyboards almost look like a comic strip version of the film; they were used extensively by Walt Disney Studios to plan animated feature films. Another example of someone who made extensive use of storyboards was the famous thriller director, Alfred Hitchcock.

The images produced for a storyboard should indicate what will be seen (mise-en-scène) and show how the film will be seen through the camera lens (cinematography). So an establishing shot of a house in the country will show a drawing or a photograph of a distant house surrounded by trees and grass. Similarly, an extreme close-up of a person screaming in a dark room will be a drawing or a photograph of a head against a dark background. In addition to this visual image, the storyboard will include a written description of the shot (a description of the mise-en-scène with reference to any camera movement within the shot) as well as other important information on sound and editing. Your storyboard should enable a director to visualise the sequence precisely so it will provide information on all the key micro aspects of film language as follows:

Aspect of Film Language	What should be considered?	How will it be shown?
Mise-en-scène	Setting, costume, lighting, props, character movement and facial expressions, make-up and lighting.	Through the images of individual shots on the storyboard. There may be further explanation in a scene description.
Cinematography	Camera angle, camera distance, camera movement and camera framing.	The individual shots on the storyboard correctly labelled. Arrows can be used for movement.

Aspect of Film Language	What should be considered?	How will it be shown?
Sound	Dialogue (voice), music and noise (atmosphere and sound effects).	Labelling to indicate what the viewer would be able to hear during every shot. Dialogue is not reproduced word for word.
Editing	Shot duration and transitions (how we cut from one shot to the next).	Every shot should be labelled with duration and any transition other than a straight cut should be identified.

Close up: the classroom

Once you have decided what kind of sequence you intend to make, you should look at similar sequences from similar films to see how aspects of film language are being used.

The best way to do this is by using a DVD or Blu-ray disc, which can be paused easily, and using a creating a simplified storyboard like the grid below.

Continue to do this for the first 10 or so shots.

Shot	Image of shot	Mise-en-scène	Cinema-tography	Sound	Editing
1	Drawing of long shot of building with trees.	Old grey building, trees sway in the wind	Long shot of old, grey building. Camera slowly tracks towards the building.	Low rumbling noise and high pitched wind howling	Duration: 4 seconds. Cut to next shot
2					
3					

Storyboards can be produced in a variety of formats as you may find when you check examples of them. However, they all have the following in common:

- the shot number

- a visual image which shows what that shot is (for example, a long shot of a house, an establishing shot or an extreme close up of a person's face)

- an indication of the length of the shot

- a description of the mise-en-scène

- identification of shot used (e.g. long shot), including reference to any camera movement within the shot

- sound details, including both diegetic and non-diegetic sound but without dialogue

- an indication of the transition to the next shot (for example, 'Cut to').

Different genres will have different ways of filming different kinds of sequence. This is based on years of industry practice, so why not draw on this experience and use similar kinds of shots. This is not to say that you copy an existing sequence – but borrow good ideas from different films so that you can show your knowledge of film language. Most sequences begin, for example, with an establishing shot and move closer to the centre of the action as the sequence continues. It is interesting to note that very common shots in films, such as over-the-shoulder shots, are hardly ever used by students when they are producing storyboards.

Close up: creative work

Plan a complete sequence, with a sense of a beginning, middle and end point. Choose significant or **pivotal** scenes from your imaginary film. It's best to plan this shot by shot before you begin to draw or photograph the shots. You could use something similar to the grid used for the preparation task. This will allow you to make sure that you are covering all of the areas of film language in a way that makes your sequence and your intended message clear.

- Try to get a variety of shots in terms of distance, angle and movement. The preparation task should help you to do this.

- Use a digital camera and photograph the shots instead of drawing the images. This often produces better results, especially if you're not very good at drawing.

- Make sure you include all of the relevant detail.

- Careful consideration of mise-en-scène is expected at the highest levels.

Magazine

There are a wide range of magazines that only focus on films and the film industry. There are general film magazines, which include features on forthcoming films and interviews with stars and directors, and there is also a range of special interest film magazines which seek to explore and engage with film on a more academic level.

Magazines can be a good way of promoting new films to an audience that is likely to be interested, as people who read film magazines tend to be those who go to the cinema regularly or buy DVDs or Blu-ray discs to enjoy at home. This can be a really clever form of marketing as it is *almost* free – the film's distributors will cover the costs of making information available and arranging for the stars to do publicity work such as interviews.

1: *Sight & Sound* magazine

2: *Empire* magazine

When you look at the covers of film magazines, it is often stars that are given centre stage, and they are used as a selling point for the magazines. More recently, big film franchises such as *X-Men* and *Transformers* have been able to take over the covers of magazines with their graphic artwork or logo.

In this task you are attempting to show your knowledge of how films are promoted through the media and you must consider the following:

The title of the magazine. The brief is for a new film magazine and you must come up with an appropriate title. This may be an opportunity to show that your magazine may be more specifically focused (perhaps focusing on one genre).

What kind of image should you use? This could be the key to success with your pre-production as magazine covers normally have carefully constructed images which relate to the film that is being promoted.

How is the film you are promoting referred to? How will you use headings and teasers on the magazine cover to attract people to read about your film?

What other features will be included? This is the opportunity to show your understanding of film magazines, the types of things they include and the way that these are used to attract audiences.

Close up: the classroom

The best preparation is to look at real film magazines. Look at the covers for 3 film magazines (these can easily be found on the internet) and work through the questions above.

Close up: creative work

- The significance of **your** film must be evident, both in the images and the text.

- Are there more interesting ways the cover could be used, such as gatefold covers (which fold out into larger images) or even two alternative covers for the same issue of a magazine which focus on different stars or aspect of the film?

Marketing Campaign

Marketing is usually the responsibility of the film's distributor, but the process may begin before a single shot has been filmed. If you choose to produce the marketing campaign the possibilities are endless, and you should spend time looking at the ways films being released at the moment are marketed.

You must produce at least 4 items and may consider some of the following:

Teaser poster

These are posters produced which give away very little about the film, and are visibly different from those used once the film is about to be released. They will usually contain the film's artwork and a suggestion of when it is likely to be released. In some cases, where there is existing awareness of the franchise, the teaser poster may just include the logo (Superman and Batman logos were used very effectively when the franchises were brought back to life a few years ago). Most teaser posters consist of one strong central image or graphic, a tagline and a vague date such as 'This Summer' or even just a year ('2013').

3: The Dark Knight Rises (2012) teaser poster, released a whole year before the film

Screen saver/wallpaper

These are images which can be downloaded and used as the background to your computer or mobile phone, or to be displayed when the device is idle. They will usually consist of an image and the film's artwork and may be variations on the teaser poster. These are useful as they will be seen many times by the person who has chosen them as well as others (friends and family members).

Display items for the cinema

These days, cardboard standees compete for our attention at the cinema and they can be over 2 metres tall and even wider. They are much bigger than posters and are usually 3-dimensional so they have more impact than traditional posters. If you choose to include these in your marketing campaign annotated designs are acceptable.

Tie-in products

Tie-in products are usually 'special edition' versions of products that are already available. This could be something as simple as a drinks can which uses images and artwork from a new film. Disney has been particularly successful in this area and images from most new Disney films can be seen on the box of a Happy Meal at McDonalds at the time of release with the bonus of a film themed toy.

Merchandise

These are products linked to the film intended for sale, and could be anything from a baseball cap to an action figure. Fantasy, science fiction and Superhero movies are particularly suited to this kind of product, but any genre could be used.

Viral adverts

These have emerged over the last 10 years in response to the growth of the internet and the fear that younger audiences may not respond to traditional forms of marketing. These are adverts which do not necessarily give away the identity of the film; they may not even look like adverts and are designed to get people onto the web researching the film. They could be related to publicity stunts (events staged to raise a film's profile). They can be a great way of getting cheap marketing for new films that do not have the distribution budget of the big Hollywood summer blockbusters, and films such as *Paranormal Activity* (2007) owe their success to this kind or marketing.

Whichever you choose, you really must look into examples and consider how to best use the chosen medium. Don't just assume you know what a viral advert is – research successful film viral marketing campaigns.

Close up: the classroom

Using a popular shopping website, such as Amazon.com, search for a popular film franchise such as Indiana Jones or Harry Potter. Answer the following questions:

- What items are available?
- What do they tell you about the target audience?
- Why would consumers be interested in buying these items?

Close up: creative work

- Make sure that the artwork is consistent.
- Make sure items of merchandise are appropriate for the type of film you are making and, more importantly, the target audience.
- Try to create a variety of marketing items for your campaign – teaser posters, posters, viral advertising or items of merchandise.

Production

Production is the major controlled assessment component and should really pull together different areas of learning from the course. Whichever product you choose to produce, you must show that you can demonstrate:

- Research, planning and presentation skills.
- Creative and technical skills.
- Knowledge and understanding of how films communicate with the audience.

The work will be assessed with these things in mind.

You must develop the idea from your pre-production and both your pre-production and your production must be based on the same film idea you created for your pitch.

Suggested combinations:

Pre-production	Production
Screenplay	Short sequence
Storyboard	Press pack
Magazine cover and contents	Website
Marketing campaign	Magazine feature article

Combinations to avoid:

Pre-production	Production
Magazine cover	Magazine feature
Marketing campaign	Poster campaign

Film Sequence

The filmed sequence is the best way to demonstrate what you have learned in relation to film language elsewhere on the course as it requires you to plan, film and edit a short sequence that creates tension and/or atmosphere. This option is available as a solo project or a group project.

The sequence can be from any point in your imaginary film and could be the first 2 minutes of what you plan to be a much longer sequence. The best examples do not usually go over the 2 minute mark; however, they show clear understanding of how the following features can be effectively used to create meaning:

- Mise-en-scène
- Camera/cinematography
- Sound
- Editing.

The list above should also give you a good idea about what different roles are available for the members of your group.

Group work

It is advised that you work in a group for this project, and although you might be keen to work alone, it can be very time consuming and demanding and may be best discussed with your teacher.

It is important that every member of your group has a specific role as their mark will be related to their contribution in this area. It is not enough to say 'we all worked together' as this makes it very difficult to see who has done what. For this reason the role of **director** is not really an option. Although a director's role is vital in the real industry, it can be hard to judge the director's contribution, as they oversee all of the other areas. There are 4 clearly defined roles and depending on the size of your group, you should distribute these between the group members. Below are a some suggestions of how you might organise this:

Group of 2

Student A	Mise-en-scène, Camera/Cinematography
Student B	Sound, Editing

Group of 3

Student A	Mise-en-scène, Camera/Cinematography
Student B	Sound, Editing
Student C	Sound, Editing

Group of 4

Student A	Mise-en-scène, Camera/Cinematography
Student B	Sound, Camera/Cinematography
Student C	Mise-en-scène, Editing
Student D	Sound, Editing

For each of the different roles there are specific things that you need to make sure you consider. This will not only show the knowledge that you have acquired elsewhere on the course, but also create greater opportunities for you to get the higher level marks.

Mise-en-scène

This role would be covered by a large number of people on a real film, from prop designers to set dressers and costume designers, as well as the director (who essentially pulls together the different aspects at the time of filming). To get the highest marks you must show that you have creatively controlled the following aspects of the film's visuals but we would expect you to combine this with another responsibility:

Location – Where are you going to film? Why is this a suitable location? How will it affect the response of the audience?

Set Dressing – How will you 'style' the location that you have chosen? How will this help the audience to understand what is going on? Done well you can turn the least promising filming locations (such as a classroom) into many different places, but you must pay attention to detail. The audience will never believe your classroom is a police station if there is a wall display with 'GCSE English Language' in the background.

Props – What props would the audience expect to see in this kind of sequence? Are these available or will they have to be made?

Lighting – What control do you have over the lighting? How could this be used to create atmosphere?

Costume – What does this tell us about the characters? Are the costumes used appropriate?

Camerawork/Cinematography

Simply filming the events that take place in the sequence is not enough to get you into the higher mark bands as the camera can be used in much more creative ways to create atmosphere in a film. The best candidates are able to show that they have control over the following:

Camera Distance – Try to include a range of appropriate shots from those that are very close, to those that are further away. An establishing shot is a good starting point for any sequence. You should also avoid using too many of the same type of shot (mid-shot for instance).

Camera Angle – look for opportunities to include a greater range of angles and avoid shooting the whole thing at eye-level. Try to include at least one high and one low angle in the sequence.

Camera Movement – This may be difficult if you do not have access to very much equipment. It is advisable to use a tripod at all times unless you are trying to achieve a specific effect. Any tripod will allow you to tilt and pan, but the zoom is probably best avoided as it is difficult to use well.

Focus – You must make sure that the footage that makes it into the finished sequence is in focus (unless there is a clearly justified reason for out of focus shots). If you are using a camera with an automatic focus you should avoid sudden movements and try out different lighting levels when you are filming.

Sound

The soundtrack is often overlooked in student productions, but done well this can be one of the more important areas to contribute to the atmosphere of the sequence. It is vital that the sound is considered at the planning stage, even if it will be created during the edit, as it is obvious when sound has not been given proper attention. The following aspects must be considered:

Dialogue – There is no requirement for you to have dialogue in the sequence, but if you do you must make sure that it is clear. You should also think about the other ways that dialogue could be included, perhaps adding a voice-over.

Music – This could be a key area where you underline the atmosphere created visually with appropriately chosen music. In a real film, this is likely to be written specifically for the sequence (a film score), and will not usually have lyrics. For this reason you should try to find music that is instrumental and make decisions based upon suitability – not just songs that you like. You should also think about when the music should come in and fade out: playing 2 minutes of music at the same volume throughout the sequence does not really show creativity or technical ability and could lose you marks if this is your area of responsibility.

Sound Effects – You really need to think about how the simplest sounds contribute to the overall meaning in the sequence. In a real film most of the sounds that we hear have been created separately by the **Foley artist** and added during post-production. You should think about what sounds the audience would expect to hear (this could be something as simple as footsteps) and make sure that these are audible in the finished sequence. You may need to record these separately or you could search for sound effects using the internet.

> **Key terms**
>
> **Foley artist:** Person responsible for creating everyday sounds in films (named after Jack Foley, who first produced these in 1927).

Editing

The editor is responsible for pulling the other aspects together. It is a big role and the overall success of the sequence can be entirely dependent on this. The following need to be considered:

Shot duration – This needs to be long enough so that the audience can see what is going on, but not so long that the audience is waiting for the next shot. Traditionally, the longer shots are at the start of the sequence and the shots get progressively shorter as the sequence reaches its climax.

Transitions – In most cases, as in the majority of films, you will use straight cuts when moving from one shot to the next. If you want to use a different kind of transition, then be sure it is the right one for the atmosphere that you are trying to create. Including lots of different kinds of transitions will distract the audience and does not get you any additional marks!

Web Page

Almost all films – regardless of budget – will have an 'official website' which will be used to market the film in advance of its release. These often stay 'live' for years and can be a place for fans of the films to share their thoughts or buy merchandise. This may be in addition to the use of other social networking sites such as **Facebook** and **Twitter** and although you may want to incorporate references to these sites, the task is to create the official website for your imaginary film.

Websites are carefully tailored to appeal to specific groups and the appearance and contents will differ depending on the film's genre and target audience. They commonly include the following:

- The film's logo (on every page).
- An 'about the movie' page with a synopsis and other details on the film.
- Videos – trailers, clips from the film, 'behind the scenes' featurettes and interviews.
- Gallery – Images from the film, production stills and publicity photographs of the actors.
- Characters – profiles of the major characters.
- Downloads – wallpaper for your PC/Mac/Smartphone, ringtones.
- The URL (web address) for official sites is usually www._____movie. com (so a film called *The Babysitter* would have the URL www. thebabysittermovie.com).

Promotional websites will normally follow the following structure:

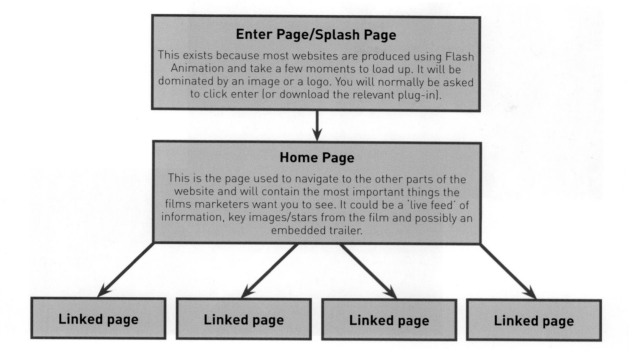

Preparation Task

The best preparation for this task is to look at as many different film websites as possible, listing the types of things that are contained. Use the following grid as a guide:

Images	How many? What are they of? What is the balance between images from the film and those that we would class as publicity images?
Artwork	How significant is the logo and how is it used across the website?
Style	How does the website use colour and different fonts? How is each page set out – is there a consistent style? How does the style of the website relate to the film's genre?
Contents	What pages are there? What is the balance between text and image? What type of information is being included? What are the major similarities with the others you have looked at? Are there any differences?

Case Study *X-Men: First Class* website

4: X-Men: First Class website

Splash Page

Against a black background a white 'X' begins to grow from the middle. There is no other text on the page and nothing to click at this stage. It takes approximately 30 seconds for the 'X' to grow to full size and we are taken to the home page (we do not need to click).

Home Page

The home page is also black. It has a Twitter feed at the top along with the familiar Twitter and Facebook logos; there are also controls for screen size and audio. The navigation bar sits at the bottom of the page and moves when you roll over the icons with your mouse; it also makes a 'file scanning' noise as though you are looking at Top Secret documents. At the centre of the page is the film's logo. At the very bottom are the recognisable production company logos for Marvel and 20th Century Fox. These elements (navigation bar and logo) remain constant as you navigate between the different pages of the site. The film's trailer automatically plays on the home page in a large central window. When the trailer has finished the background is similar to the splash page, with the 'X' now taking on the appearance of doors to a vault.

Music from the film is played in the background; it is an instrumental piece that sets an atmosphere of conspiracy and intrigue. There are also occasional 'sound bites' from the film with characters saying things like 'A new species is being born'. After around 30 seconds the background images change and the 'X doors' open to reveal still images of the central characters and moving images from the film, in the background, in the four corners created by the opening of the 'X doors'.

About the movie

The background of this page is dominated by a publicity image of Charles Xavier (James McAvoy) looking thoughtful. The film is summarised in a simple one paragraph synopsis. It doesn't give away much about the film and is more like the type of synopsis that you would get on the back of a DVD box rather than the one used for your pitch, which gives away the whole narrative. It also makes reference to the success of the *X-Men* franchise.

Downloads

The downloads page has a large image of Emma Frost (January Jones). There are only three options: Wallpaper, Twitter Skins and Icons. These are all images taken directly from the film that can be saved free of charge. The sound effects used on the home page are used when you roll over the small icons which indicate the images that are available for download.

Gallery

The gallery contains six high resolution images from the film. These are production stills and are used to tell different aspects of the narrative. Each one focuses on a different character or aspect of the film. They also give clear ideas about production design as sets and costume can be seen in detail.

Characters

The character page has 14 tiles with images of the major characters from the film. There is also a tile for 'crew'. Each of these can be clicked on and more information on the character is given along with a key image of them and the name of the actor. There are other options where you can click 'powers' to see what special powers the characters in the film have. You can also click 'actor' for a filmography of that particular performer.

Video

This has a large image of an action sequence from the film and three icons which link to pop-up video sequences from the film. All three icons can be seen and these focus on different aspects of the film.

Summary

Overall the website is very consistent in terms of style and has a metallic sheen which we could see as iconographic of the science fiction genre. It uses many images from the film and tries to give the audience the impression that they are getting 'Top Secret' information on the film that others do not have access to. The site makes use of lots of sound effects and audio clips from the film as well as multimedia elements (animation and video) to give the feel that you are actively engaging with the website and not just reading and looking at pictures.

Close up: creative work

- Include as many original images as you can and try to get a mixture of publicity photographs and images from the film.

- Make sure there is a consistency of style across all of your pages.

- Look at plenty of 'official' film websites and apply your findings.

- Presentation can be in print form, but make sure you annotate the images to indicate if there any animated elements, clips or sounds.

Magazine Feature

In the pre-production section we mentioned the importance of the magazine industry in keeping the audience informed of films that are in production or soon to be released. The content of magazines relies heavily on material that is supplied or made available to them by the film's marketing team who will cover the cost of supplying information and even access to stars and director. This might seem like a costly business, but a full page advert in one of the popular film magazines can be surprisingly expensive, whereas a double page interview with a star where the film is frequently mentioned could cost the distributor very little and may be more effective in getting audiences to seek out the film when it is released.

It is also not unusual to have films mentioned several times in an issue of a magazine as there may be different kinds of articles relating to one film.

You should consider what kind of article it is that you are going to produce:

- Star interview

- Profile of the star

- Production or 'on-set' report.

These are likely to cast only a positive light on the film being discussed, as negative publicity on a star might mean that the magazine does not get an interview in the future and many magazines rely upon stars to draw in their readers.

Whichever you choose, the significance of your film must be evident.

Close up: creative work

- Look at the ways magazines include additional information on the star/film and try to replicate this.

- Make sure there are a range of relevant images, and avoid using any found images.

- Make sure images used are appropriate (a picture of you on the school corridor captioned 'the director' doesn't suggest you have planned it very well).

Poster Campaign

Almost all new films released have a poster at the core of the marketing campaign and variations of this will appear at cinemas, in newspapers and magazines, as well as on billboards, bus stops and the side of buses. The poster is arguably the original form of film marketing as it has been around for such a long time and is likely to be the most visible item leading up to the release of a new film.

When planning the poster the key things you should be trying to get across to the audience are:

- Stars – and the type of character they will play.

- Genre – using key conventions or iconography.

- Narrative – even if it is just an idea of what the film is about (the premise).

Most posters contain the following:

Artwork – the film's logo, designed in a specific way. The style will usually be a clear indicator of genre.

Stars – Images of the stars as well as star names (usually with the emphasis on the star's surname).

Tag line – a short sentence giving an overall idea of what the film is about.

Release date – this may be specific ('August 1st') or seasonal ('This Summer').

Credit Band – details of the key people involved in the production. There are specific conventions for this and certain fonts that allow you to recreate these – it's worth searching the internet for ideas on this.

The best preparation for this task is to look at lots of posters. Very often candidates launch into the production of posters because they think they know exactly what needs to be included, but posters are quite a specific text and it can be easy to miss the point.

Close up: the classroom

Compare two posters for films from a genre similar to your own idea.

Make notes on a grid like the one below:

	Poster A	Poster B
Images What are the main images? What do they tell you about character, genre and narrative? How is colour used? What size are the images? How are the images combined?		
Text What different kinds of information are on the poster? What font/typeface is used and what does it signify/suggest? How are text and image incorporated?		

Close up: creative work

- Make sure that there is enough variation between the posters you produce.

- Aim for consistency in terms of style and artwork – you don't want them to look like posters for completely different films. If you are going to change the artwork/logo, think about why.

- Be creative with your original images.

- Make sure that star, genre and basic premise are clear.

Press Pack

In some ways the press pack is the most flexible of the production briefs as it could cover a range of material. Press packs are usually supplied to the press (newspapers, magazines, TV and the internet) ahead of a film's release, giving key information about the film which could be turned into a news item, or used when reviewing the film. In the past these would have been posted to all of the major news organisations, though these days it is done digitally.

Therefore, at the core of the press pack there should be a **press release** which takes the form of an open letter drawing the readers' attention to key details about the film (its premise/storyline, the stars and the background to the production). These will usually be 300–500 words and may use things like bold text to grab the attention of the journalist who may be looking for things to say about the film.

Another key aspect of the press pack will be **production stills** which are a compulsory component if you choose this option. These will be images from the film that can be reproduced by the press. They will include key images which tell part of the story and are supplied with a caption to explain what is going on. These are not simply screen shots from the film, but will have been carefully constructed by the film's publicity department. You should look back at your notes on mise-en-scène and make sure that you consider all of the visual features such as costume and setting before picking up a camera. Traditionally film stills were 10x8 inches (25.4cm x 20.32cm) on photographic paper, but these days the press would expect a high resolution image that can be reproduced clearly.

5: This production still for *Iron Man* shows the director, Jon Favreau, conversing with star Robert Downey Jnr. on the set

The other information included in the press pack could encompass items such as film posters, interviews with stars and directors and sequences from the film, which also appear in other options.

Close up: creative work

- Carefully consider the type of information that you want to include.

- Highlight any of your film's unique selling points (USPs) that might get the press to write about your film. This could be that the film has been made by a first time director, or that the star of your film won an Oscar for their last performance; it could even be the suggestion of a romance on set.

- Spend time carefully planning your film stills and make sure that they say something about your film (which a picture of you smiling at the camera in your school/college corridor will not).

Evaluative Analysis

The evaluative analysis requires you to reflect back on the success of your production, but also gets you to think about how the decisions you made have affected the overall success of the finished product.

It does not have to be a written analysis and may take the form of a presentation or report, but the following things must be covered:

Technical and creative skills – how successful is the finished product in terms of what you were trying to do? You might want to include reference to some real products and make a brief comparison. This should relate to your role if you worked in a group.

Format – did you include the appropriate conventions for whatever you produced? Again, a brief comparison with, for example, a similar website or magazine feature, would help you check that.

Film language – what have you learnt about the way film language is used from your production work? As all of the products are visual, you should be able to discuss some aspect of mise-en-scène. Some of the options may suit themselves to a discussion of organisations and audiences. If you worked in a group to produce a film sequence, your evaluative analysis should primarily discuss your area of responsibility (for example, sound or camerawork).

Organisations and audiences – what have you learnt about organisations and audiences from your production? Was there one key thing you learnt about the film industry – for example the importance of marketing or branding? How did your production target its audience? How would the audience respond to your product? You may want to discuss one element (a shot of the artwork) and discuss the kind of response this is meant to get. You may consider asking your friends and family for some feedback on this.

Glossary

Anti-Semitism: prejudice against Jewish people.

Archetype: an instantly recognisable representation of a character that has been in use for a very long time.

Artwork: although 'artwork' refers to any graphic design work, in film it tends to refer to a film's logo, which will be designed in a particular way and does not change. In the case of film franchises the artwork may be reused over a number films, think of the *Harry Potter* artwork with its lightning bolt 'P', or the logo's for *Transformers* and *Batman*.

Audience: a group of people with similar tastes and/or characteristics.

'A' List: the list of stars that are currently attracting the highest salaries and most prestigious film deals.

Backers: the companies or individuals who provide money to fund a film's production.

Binary opposite: a conflict between two opposing ideas or characters, at the root of most popular narratives. This conflict, for example between good and evil, is generally resolved at the end of the narrative.

BBFC: British Board of Film Classification. The industry body responsible for classifying films and advising on the content of these classifications.

Blockbuster: a film that takes over $100 million at the US box office.

Box Office: the money a film generates in ticket sales. A reference to where people traditionally buy their tickets.

'B' Movie: lower budget films, or those made for TV or which go straight to DVD.

Chronological: arranged in the order of time.

Cinematography: camera framing, camera movement and lighting. In film production, lighting is the responsibility of the 'cinematographer' – the Director of Photography. In studying film, lighting is often considered part of mise-en-scene, as we have done in this book.

Civilisation: a society in an advanced state of social development.

Close Up Shot: when we are close up to a subject so we can focus on a face, or an object in detail.

Codes and Conventions: the typical 'rules' of the genre – the micro and macro aspects expected by an audience.

Computer generated imagery (CGI): how visual effects are created using computer technology in 'post-production (see 'visual effects').

Conglomerate: a huge business formed by the buying up of smaller businesses.

Connotation: the meanings that are suggested by what we see and hear on the screen.

Continuity Editing: the editing style designed to be invisible. Transitions are constructed to be as smooth as possible to ensure the audience is fully absorbed in the unfolding story.

Cross-Cutting: cutting between different sets of action that can be happening at the same time or at different times.

DC Comics (originally 'Detective Comics'): one of the two largest publishers of comics, established, like Marvel, in the 1930s.

Denotation: what we actually see or hear on the screen.

Development Hell: an informal way of describing an idea or a script that has spent a long time 'stuck' in the very early stages of pre-production, often years.

Dialogue: conversations between characters.

Distribution: the processes involved in getting a film to an audience.

Editing: the process by which shots are put together into sequences or scenes. Usually described according to rhythm or pace (i.e. the varying lengths of the shots in the sequence) and type of transition (e.g. cut, fade, dissolve or mix, wipe).

Ellipsis: events that are missed out of a narrative as they are not needed for plot development.

Exhibition: where and how films are shown.

Fable: a fictional story which contains some kind of moral message.

Fans: the audience that has a greater level of involvement or interest in a film than the average spectator.

Film Industry (or Film Business): the commercial aspect of making films – production, distribution and exhibition.

Film Language: the ways in which a film communicates to its audience.

Film Rights: the legal permission to use another parties copyrighted characters(s) in a film.

Flashback: when we see a scene from the past that is somehow relevant to the narrative in the present.

Foley Artist: Foley is the reproduction of everyday sounds for use in film- making. These reproduced sounds can be anything from the swishing of clothing and footsteps to squeaky doors and breaking glass.

Formulaic: where a film contains the same ingredients as others.

Franchise: where a film and its often planned sequels are part of a larger business entity.

Generic Conventions: the various ways in which film language is typically used within particular genres.

Generic Type: a certain personality or type of person seen repeatedly in a particular genre.

Genocide: the deliberate extermination of a people or nation.

Genre: a type or category.

Hand-Held Camera: the camera is held manually. Shots are therefore unclear as the camera is held without support.

High Angle Shot: when a camera is positioned above people or objects, they generally look smaller and so more vulnerable.

High Concept Pitch: a pitch for a film based on a very basic narrative idea. They will often rely on special effects and stars to make the concept work.

High Key Lighting: bright lighting, the addition of lots of artificial ('filler') light to a scene.

Holocaust: the name given to the Nazis' attempt to wipe out the Jewish race.

Hybrid Genre: where characteristics from two different genres are put together in one film.

Iconic: a readily recognizable image with commonly held associations.

Iconography: objects, images, characters etc. strongly associated with a particular genre. E.g. spaceships and sci-fi, cowboys and the western.

Ideology: refers to a group's, an individual's, or a country's values and beliefs.

Independent: smaller companies that operate outside of the control of the larger conglomerates.

Licence: the agreement that allows one company to use another's property. It will involve a fee and/or a profit share.

Log Line: a one sentence summary of a film.

Long Shot: when we are a distance away from the subject so all of it is visible and maybe more of the setting and other people.

Loss Leader: a product sold at a loss by a business to promote the sale of its other products.

Low Angle Shot: if the camera is positioned below a subject looking up, it looks larger and more powerful.

Low Key Lighting: where fewer 'filler' lights are used creating shadows and pools of darkness.

Macguffin: an object the securing of which drives the narrative forward, a definition credited to Alfred Hitchcock: 'The object around which the plot revolves, but, as to what that object specifically is, the audience don't care.'

Mainstream Audience: the largest film audience that sees most of its films at a multiplex.

Marketing: the process of finding out what people want, developing a product to meet this desire and then selling it to them.

Marvel Comics: the largest of the big 2 American comic book publishers (along with DC Comics).

Merchandise: products you can buy based on the film, many in number, ranging from toys, through souvenirs through clothing to expensive prop replicas.

Micro Features: mise-en-scène, cinematography, sound and editing.

Montage Sequence: a series of shots which summarise an action or build a mood, rather than playing it out in the equivalent of real time. (Source: BFI)

Multiplex: a cinema with a large number of screens.

Multi-Platform: properties that appear in more than one format, e.g. comics, films, TV, games.

Narrative: the film's story and the way in which it is told.

Narrative Structure: the way in which the narrative is ordered and organised within a film.

Narrative Voice-Over: the use of an unseen narrator to tell the audience parts of the film's story.

Negotiated Reading: when you read some of the ideas that are intended but do not see, or agree with others.

Omniscient Narrative: where the audience know more than the characters about narrative events and plot details.

Opening Weekend: the money a film takes in its first weekend of release.

Oppositions: where characters personify two aspects of the same idea, or two 'sides of the same coin'. For example predator & prey.

Oppositional Reading: when you disagree with the film's messages and values.

Original Screenplay: a script for a film based on a 'new' idea and not an existing property.

Package: a deal put together by a producer that contains the main elements of a film; a property, director, star(s). They can then 'sell' this package to investors to secure finance.

Parallel Editing: cuts that are designed to show us different events that are going on at the same time within a narrative.

Parallel Narratives: when two or more characters share different stories that centre on the same event.

Pitch: a short presentation of ideas for a film delivered to an agent or producer.

Plot: the more detailed plan of how the story is to be told in a film. Effectively how all the scenes of a film, which make up its plot, are constructed through editing.

Plot Points: the major events that take place in a film which help to shape the film's narrative.

Preferred Reading: when your reading of the film is what the director was intending.

Premiere: the first screening of a film in a country. Typically it will take place in the capitol or a major city. The stars will be present and much publicity is generated from their trip down the red carpet.

Print: the copy of a film shown in cinemas. From 2013, celluloid prints will be replaced by digital copies of film (effectively high quality DVDs).

Production: the activity of organizing the practical and financial matters connected with the making of a film.

Product Placement: when a film features products and brands prominently in return for a fee or sponsorship.

Propaganda: publicity designed to confirm religious or political beliefs.

Property: any source of ideas that has been used to create a film.

Realism: a believable representation of events.

Release Pattern: how often and where a film will be shown. General release is as wide as possible, limited release may only be London or specialist cinemas.

Representation: how people, groups, races or religions are presented on screen – the 'image' given to them through the way they are portrayed.

Restricted Narrative: a narrative where we know only as much as the characters in the film.

Re-Boot: when or a comic or franchise is started again almost from scratch without reference to the previous version(s).

Rights: the legal permission that allows on person to use another's ideas.

Rite Of Passage: a ritual or event which marks a change in an individual (as from adolescence to adulthood).

Significant Prop: an object in a scene that our attention is drawn to because it is going to become of significance later on in the film.

Social Realism: a style of film-making that deals with social issues and uses particular filmic techniques.

Sound or Soundtrack: the sounds that can be heard in a film - dialogue, sound effects, music.

Sound Bridge: when a scene begins with the carry-over sound from the previous scene before the new sound begins.

Special Effects: those traditional physical effects such as stunts and explosions.

Spheres Of Action: the place, range, or extent of what is happening at particular points in a story.

Spin-Offs: when a film leads to other related projects e.g. films, computer games, TV shows.

Star: an actor who has their own audience beyond the parts they play. Their presence in a film may guarantee a good sized audience.

Star Vehicle: a film marketed and made to 'show off' the qualities that made the particular star attractive to their target audience.

Steadicam: a camera mounted on a harness that is then attached to camera operator, so the movement of the camera is smooth.

Stereotype: a simplified representation of a person or group of people, repeatedly used so it becomes seen as the norm.

Stereotypical Representation: a simplistic way of representing people, places or social groups.

Stock Characters & Stereotypes: simple characters that are only very superficial and depend on our knowledge of clichés to recognise them.

Sub Genre: where a grouping of films with even more specialist characteristics develops within a larger genre...a genre within a genre. E.g. The Zombie film is a horror sub-genre.

Swastika: the symbol of Nazi Germany.

Symbolic: an image or object which has additional meaning or cultural significance.

Themes: the ideas suggested by films - particular genres are often associated with particular themes.

The Final Solution: the Nazi plan to kill every Jew in Europe.

Tie-Ins: an individual piece of a franchise directly related to the film.

Typical: displaying an expected feature e.g. a typical feature of the Superhero genre is...

USP: Unique Selling Point. A marketing term for focusing on the feature of your product that sets it apart from its competitors.

Verisimilitude: the appearance of reality. The quality of a film that allows the audience to accept it could happen.

Viral Marketing: internet based promotion that depends on the audience 'passing it on' and getting involved for its effectiveness.

Visual Effects: images created in post-production using computer technology often referred to as CGI (computer generated imagery).

Voice-Over: when a character from the film or an unknown voice gives us additional information over the top of the action of the film.

Going further: books and websites used in the preparation of this book

Film Language

Reading films: Key concepts for analysing film and television, Jackie Newman and Roy Stafford, bfi Education, 2002

Film Language: Study Guide, Anita Russell, Film Education

Film Art: An Introduction (7th edition), Bordwell and Thompson, McGraw-Hill. David Bordwell, 2005

AS Film Studies, Casey Benyahia, Gaffney and White, 2nd edition, Routledge, 2008

Superhero genre

Superheroes! Capes and Crusaders in Comics and Films, Roz Kaveney, I.B.Tauris, 2007

Superhero Movies, Liam Burke, Pocket Essentials, 2008

The Rough Guide to Superheroes, Helen Rodiss, Paul Simpson, Michaela Bushell, Rough Guides, 2004

Comic Book Movies - Virgin Film, David Hughes, Virgin Books, 2007

Film and Comic Books, Ian Gordon, Mark Jancovich, Matthew McAllister, University Press of Mississippi, 2007

Excelsior: The Amazing Life Of Stan Lee, Stan Lee and George Mair, Boxtree Ltd., 2002

www.brandchannel.com

www.comicbookmovie.com

www.superherohype.com

www.davidbordwell.net/blog/2008/08/16/superheroes-for-sale

www.cinemaroll.com/cinemarolling/superhero-genre-the-sub-genre-of-the-action-film

www.superheromovies.net

www.cinemablend.com

Films outside Hollywood: *The Boy in the Striped Pyjamas* and *Rabbit-Proof Fence*

The Boy in the Striped Pyjamas, John Boyne, David Fickling Books, 2006

Rabbit-Proof Fence, Doris Pilkington Garimara, Miramax Books, 2002

'In Search of an Australian Soul: Reflections on Religion and Spirituality in *Rabbit-Proof Fence* and Japanese Story,' Suzanne Langford: www.escholarship.usyd.edu

Helen Grace: 'Rabbit-Proof Fence: The Journey of Feeling,' *Australian Screen Education*, 36, 2004 (Spring)

'Long Road Home: Phillip Noyce's *Rabbit-Proof Fence*', Fiona A. Villella, www.sensesofcinema.com

The Boy in the Striped Pyjamas: Study Guide, www.filmeducation.org

Rabbit-Proof Fence: Study Unit, www.curriculumsupport.education.nsw.gov.au

Rabbit-Proof Fence, Global Film Studies Guide, www.diceproject.org

Rabbit-Proof Fence: Study guide, www.fileheap.com

Stills copyright information